Math Achievement
Enriching Activities Based on NCTM Standards

Grade 3

by
Tracy Dankberg, Jennifer Moore, and Leland Graham

Table of Contents

Introduction 3
Pretests 4-7
Answer Key for Pretests 8

Number Sense
Place Value 9
Reading and Writing Numbers 10
Expanded Notation 11
Comparing and Ordering Numbers 12
Rounding to the Nearest 10 13
Rounding to the Nearest 100 14
Problem Solving 15

Addition
Basic Addition Facts 16
Addition without Regrouping 17
Addition with Regrouping 18
Adding with Two or More Addends 19
Rounding and Estimating Sums 20
Estimating Sums 21
Problem Solving with Addition 22

Subtraction
Basic Subtraction Facts 23
Subtraction without Regrouping 24
Subtraction with Regrouping 25
Subtracting with Zero 26
Subtracting Large Numbers 27
Subtraction Practice 28
Problem Solving with Subtraction 29

Multiplication
Multiplication Facts 0-5 30
Multiplication Facts 6-9 31
Mastering Multiplication Facts 32
Multiplying One- and Two-Digit Numbers ... 33
Multiplying One- and Three-Digit Numbers .. 34
Multiplying Two- and Three-Digit Numbers ... 35
Multiplication Rounding and Estimating 36
Estimating Products with Multiplication 37
Problem Solving with Multiplication 38

Division
Division Facts 0-1 39
Division Facts 2-4 40
Division Facts 5-7 41
Division Facts 8-9 42
Division Mixed Practice 43

Division with No Remainders 44
Division with Remainders 45
Estimating Quotients 46
Problem Solving with Division 47

Fractions
Parts of a Whole 48
Parts of a Group 49
Comparing Fractions 50
Fractional Parts 51
Adding and Subtracting Fractions 52
Problem Solving with Fractions 53

Decimals
Decimal Place Value 54
Reading and Writing Decimals 55
Comparing and Ordering Decimals 56
Adding and Subtracting Decimals 57
Problem Solving with Decimals 58

Calendar and Time
Time to the Quarter Hour 59
Elapsed Time 60
Reading a Calendar 61
Problem Solving with Time 62

Money
Adding and Subtracting Money 63
Making Change under $1 64
Making Change over $1 65
Problem Solving with Money 66

Measurement
Metric Length 67
Customary Length 68
Metric Capacity and Mass 69
Customary Capacity and Mass 70
Problem Solving with Measurement 71

Geometry
Symmetry 72
Congruent Figures 73
Lines, Segments, and Rays 74
Area and Perimeter 75
Making Tables and Graphs 76
Outcomes 77
Problem Solving with Data, Graphs,
    Probability, and Statistics 78
Answer Key 79-96

Introduction

Welcome to the **Math Achievement** series! Each book in this series is designed to reinforce the math skills appropriate for each grade level and to encourage high-level thinking and problem-solving skills. Enhancing students' thinking and problem-solving abilities can help them succeed in all academic areas. In addition, experiencing success in math can increase a student's confidence and self-esteem, both in and out of the classroom.

Each **Math Achievement** book offers challenging questions **based on the standards specified by the National Council of Teachers of Mathematics (NCTM).** All five content standards (number and operations, algebra, geometry, measurement, data analysis and probability) and the process standard, problem solving, are covered in the activities.

The questions and format are similar to those found on standardized math tests. The experience students gain from answering questions in this format may help increase their test scores.

> The following math skills are covered in this book:
>
> - **problem solving**
> - **place value**
> - **rounding**
> - **estimation**
> - **addition**
> - **subtraction**
> - **multiplication**
> - **division**
> - **decimals**
> - **fractions**
> - **time**
> - **money**
> - **measurement**
> - **geometry**

These exercises can be used to enhance the regular math curriculum, to individualize instruction, to provide extra practice for home schoolers, or to review skills between grades.

Each **Math Achievement** book contains **four pretests in standardized test format** at the beginning of each book. The pretests have been designed so that they may be used individually, as four stand-alone tests, or in groups. They may be used to identify students' needs in specific areas, or to compare students' math abilities at the beginning and end of the school year. **A scoring box is also included on each activity page.** This scoring box can be programmed to suit your specific classroom and student needs with total problems, total correct, and score.

Read the following problems. Circle the letter beside the correct answer.

1. 68
    + 7

A. 75
B. 78
C. 135

5. 125
    + 234

A. 472
B. 359
C. 171

9. 68
    + 54

A. 122
B. 104
C. 11

13. 635
    − 91

A. 732
B. 544
C. 626

2. 85
    + 8

A. 83
B. 93
C. 97

6. 346
    − 222

A. 554
B. 124
C. 568

10. 91
    − 78

A. 27
B. 16
C. 13

14. 252
    + 51

A. 203
B. 213
C. 303

3. 27
    − 4

A. 23
B. 42
C. 31

7. 728
    + 120

A. 848
B. 840
C. 608

11. 19
    + 12

A. 21
B. 31
C. 27

15. 172
    + 642

A. 523
B. 814
C. 810

4. 33
    − 9

A. 42
B. 22
C. 24

8. 562
    − 136

A. 426
B. 494
C. 537

12. 37
    − 17

A. 44
B. 20
C. 27

16. 840
    − 797

A. 43
B. 650
C. 937

17. Jeremy has 276 baseball cards. Marcus has 392. How many do they have altogether?

A. 698   B. 667   C. 668   D. 431

18. The school band has 143 members. Twenty-six members missed practice. How many members came to practice?

A. 121   B. 117   C. 125   D. 134

Total Problems: 18   Total Correct: 13   Score: 13/18

Name _Sara_

Read the following problems. Circle the letter beside the correct answer.

1. (circled)
```
   1,136
 + 2,073
```
A. 4,029
B. 3,109
C. 4,289
D. 3,209 (circled)

2.
```
   7,829
 - 3,827
```
A. 4,020
B. 4,002 (circled)
C. 3,982 (circled)
D. 3,829

3.
```
  38,572
+ 38,275
```
A. 76,747
B. 78,365
C. 76,847 (circled)
D. 78,292

4.
```
  72,859
- 28,349
```
A. 28,457
B. 12,938
C. 18,847
D. 44,510 (circled)

5.
```
   502
 - 121
```
A. 421
B. 381 (circled)
C. 481
D. 622

6.
```
   1,302
 -   982
```
A. 480
B. 420
C. 320 (circled)
D. 484

7.
```
   8,720
 - 1,943
```
A. 2,847
B. 2,872
C. 7,928
D. 6,777 (circled)

8.
```
   9,040
 - 1,221
```
A. 7,819 (circled)
B. 7,928 (circled)
C. 7,829
D. 8,221

9. 37 is closer to which number?

A. 40 (circled)   B. 30   C. 50

10. 62 is closer to which number?

A. 70   B. 50   C. 60 (circled)

11. 248 is closer to which number?

A. 250 (circled)   B. 240   C. 300

12. 902 is closer to which number?

A. 900 (circled)   B. 1,000 (circled)   C. 950

13. The best estimate for
56 + 42 = ____ is:

A. 100   B. 90   C. 110 (circled)

14. The best estimate for
102 + 39 = ____ is:

A. 150 (circled)   B. 100   C. 140

15. The best estimate for
68 - 22 = ____ is:

A. 50   B. 40   C. 60 (circled)

16. The best estimate for
298 - 129 = ____ is:

A. 100   B. 300   C. 200 (circled)

Total Problems: _____   **Total Correct:** _____   **Score:** _____

Read the following problems. Circle the letter beside the correct answer.

1. 3 x 7 = _____

   A. 21
   B. 24
   C. 18
   D. 36

2. 6 x 5 = _____

   A. 35
   B. 30
   C. 20
   D. 18

3. 4 x 3 = _____

   A. 12
   B. 15
   C. 18
   D. 24

4. 2 x 8 = _____

   A. 18
   B. 24
   C. 9
   D. 16

5.   10
    x 6

   A. 16
   B. 60
   C. 30
   D. 59

6.   20
    x 5

   A. 100
   B. 120
   C. 125
   D. 10

7.   23
    x 2

   A. 66
   B. 46
   C. 65
   D. 76

8.   41
    x 4

   A. 84
   B. 64
   C. 164
   D. 166

9. 3) 9

   A. 3
   B. 2
   C. 5
   D. 6

10. 2) 12

   A. 24
   B. 4
   C. 6
   D. 3

11. 6) 50

   A. 8 R2
   B. 9
   C. 7 R8
   D. 12

12. 4) 35

   A. 9 R2
   B. 7 R7
   C. 9
   D. 8 R3

13. Anne-Marie read 22 books over the summer. Each of them had about 70 pages. About how many pages did Anne-Marie read?

   A. 1,400   B. 140   C. 7,000   D. 740

14. Patrick had 36 cookies. There were 5 other boys in his study group. How many cookies did each boy get?

   A. 9   B. 6   C. 8   D. 10

| Total Problems: | Total Correct: | Score: |

Read the following problems. Circle the letter beside the correct answer.

1. What time does the clock show?

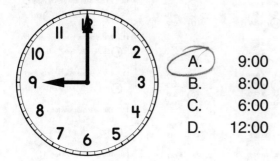

   A. 9:00
   B. 8:00
   C. 6:00
   D. 12:00

2. What time does the clock show?

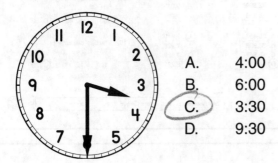

   A. 4:00
   B. 6:00
   C. 3:30
   D. 9:30

3. What time does the clock show?

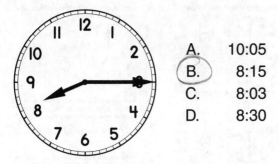

   A. 10:05
   B. 8:15
   C. 8:03
   D. 8:30

4. If the clock shows the time right now, what time will it be one hour from now?

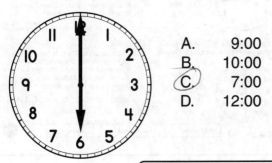

   A. 9:00
   B. 10:00
   C. 7:00
   D. 12:00

5. If the clock shows the time right now, what time was it an hour ago?

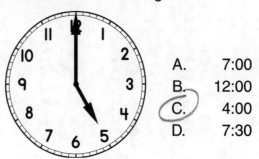

   A. 7:00
   B. 12:00
   C. 4:00
   D. 7:30

6. Ken wants to buy an ice cream cone for 75¢, a bag of potato chips for 50¢, and a drink for 95¢. How much money does he need?

   A. $3.00   B. $2.23   C. $2.20   D. $1.95

7. Keisha spent $1.35 at the school store. How much change did she get from $2.00?

   A. 65¢   B. 75¢   C. 60¢   D. 95¢

8. Nate looked under the cushion of the couch and found some change. He found 1 quarter, 3 dimes, 2 nickels, and 7 pennies. How much money did he find?

   A. $1.35   B. $2.04   C. $0.98   D. $0.72

9. Kaitlin has saved $18.25 to buy a birthday gift for her mother. She wants to buy her some perfume that costs $25.00. How much more money does Kaitlin need to save before she can buy the perfume?

   A. $7.00   B. $5.00   C. $6.25   D. $6.75

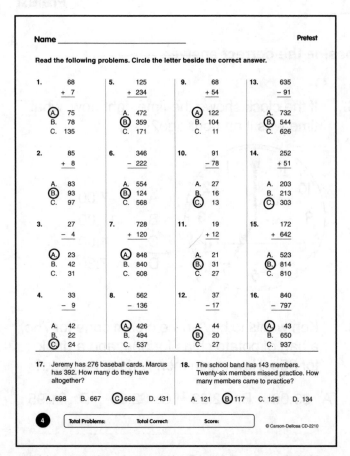

Name _____ Pretest

Read the following problems. Circle the letter beside the correct answer.

1. 68
    + 7
    Ⓐ 75
    B. 78
    C. 135

5. 125
    + 234
    A. 472
    Ⓑ 359
    C. 171

9. 68
    + 54
    Ⓐ 122
    B. 104
    C. 11

13. 635
    − 91
    A. 732
    Ⓑ 544
    C. 626

2. 85
    + 8
    A. 83
    Ⓑ 93
    C. 97

6. 346
    − 222
    A. 554
    Ⓑ 124
    C. 568

10. 91
    − 78
    A. 27
    B. 16
    Ⓒ 13

14. 252
    + 51
    A. 203
    B. 213
    Ⓒ 303

3. 27
    − 4
    Ⓐ 23
    B. 42
    C. 31

7. 728
    + 120
    Ⓐ 848
    B. 840
    C. 608

11. 19
    + 12
    A. 21
    Ⓑ 31
    C. 27

15. 172
    + 642
    A. 523
    Ⓑ 814
    C. 810

4. 33
    − 9
    A. 42
    B. 22
    Ⓒ 24

8. 562
    − 136
    Ⓐ 426
    B. 494
    C. 537

12. 37
    − 17
    A. 44
    Ⓑ 20
    C. 27

16. 840
    − 797
    Ⓐ 43
    B. 650
    C. 937

17. Jeremy has 276 baseball cards. Marcus has 392. How many do they have altogether?
    A. 698   B. 667   Ⓒ 668   D. 431

18. The school band has 143 members. Twenty-six members missed practice. How many members came to practice?
    A. 121   Ⓑ 117   C. 125   D. 134

④ Total Problems: ___ Total Correct: ___ Score: ___
© Carson-Dellosa CD-2210

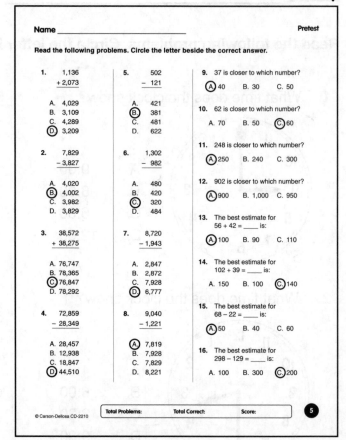

Name _____ Pretest

Read the following problems. Circle the letter beside the correct answer.

1. 1,136
    + 2,073
    A. 4,029
    B. 3,109
    C. 4,289
    Ⓓ 3,209

5. 502
    − 121
    A. 421
    Ⓑ 381
    C. 481
    D. 622

9. 37 is closer to which number?
    Ⓐ 40   B. 30   C. 50

10. 62 is closer to which number?
    A. 70   B. 50   Ⓒ 60

2. 7,829
    − 3,827
    A. 4,020
    Ⓑ 4,002
    C. 3,982
    D. 3,829

6. 1,302
    − 982
    A. 480
    B. 420
    Ⓒ 320
    D. 484

11. 248 is closer to which number?
    Ⓐ 250   B. 240   C. 300

12. 902 is closer to which number?
    Ⓐ 900   B. 1,000   C. 950

3. 38,572
    + 38,275
    A. 76,747
    B. 78,365
    Ⓒ 76,847
    D. 78,292

7. 8,720
    − 1,943
    A. 2,847
    B. 2,872
    C. 7,928
    Ⓓ 6,777

13. The best estimate for
    56 + 42 = ____ is:
    Ⓐ 100   B. 90   C. 110

14. The best estimate for
    102 + 39 = ____ is:
    A. 150   B. 100   Ⓒ 140

4. 72,859
    − 28,349
    A. 28,457
    B. 12,938
    C. 18,847
    Ⓓ 44,510

8. 9,040
    − 1,221
    Ⓐ 7,819
    B. 7,928
    C. 7,829
    D. 8,221

15. The best estimate for
    68 − 22 = ____ is:
    Ⓐ 50   B. 40   C. 60

16. The best estimate for
    298 − 129 = ____ is:
    A. 100   B. 300   Ⓒ 200

Total Problems: ___ Total Correct: ___ Score: ___   ⑤
© Carson-Dellosa CD-2210

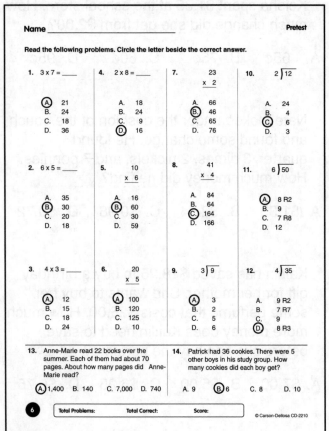

Name _____ Pretest

Read the following problems. Circle the letter beside the correct answer.

1. 3 x 7 = ____
    Ⓐ 21
    B. 24
    C. 18
    D. 36

4. 2 x 8 = ____
    A. 18
    B. 24
    C. 9
    Ⓓ 16

7. 23
    x 2
    A. 66
    Ⓑ 46
    C. 65
    D. 76

10. 2)12
    A. 24
    B. 4
    Ⓒ 6
    D. 3

2. 6 x 5 = ____
    A. 35
    Ⓑ 30
    C. 20
    D. 18

5. 10
    x 6
    A. 16
    Ⓑ 60
    C. 30
    D. 59

8. 41
    x 4
    A. 84
    B. 64
    Ⓒ 164
    D. 166

11. 6)50
    Ⓐ 8 R2
    B. 9
    C. 7 R8
    D. 12

3. 4 x 3 = ____
    Ⓐ 12
    B. 15
    C. 18
    D. 24

6. 20
    x 5
    Ⓐ 100
    B. 120
    C. 125
    D. 10

9. 3)9
    Ⓐ 3
    B. 2
    C. 5
    D. 6

12. 4)35
    A. 9 R2
    B. 7 R7
    C. 9
    Ⓓ 8 R3

13. Anne-Marie read 22 books over the summer. Each of them had about 70 pages. About how many pages did Anne-Marie read?
    Ⓐ 1,400   B. 140   C. 7,000   D. 740

14. Patrick had 36 cookies. There were 5 other boys in his study group. How many cookies did each boy get?
    A. 9   Ⓑ 6   C. 8   D. 10

⑥ Total Problems: ___ Total Correct: ___ Score: ___
© Carson-Dellosa CD-2210

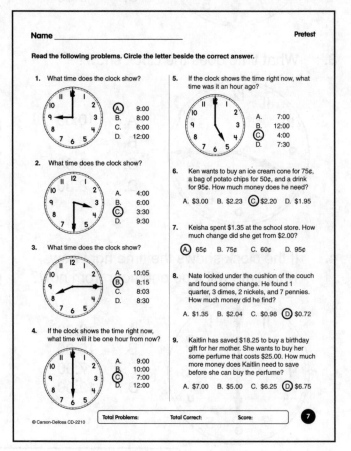

Name _____ Pretest

Read the following problems. Circle the letter beside the correct answer.

1. What time does the clock show?
    Ⓐ 9:00
    B. 8:00
    C. 6:00
    D. 12:00

5. If the clock shows the time right now, what time was it an hour ago?
    A. 7:00
    B. 12:00
    Ⓒ 4:00
    D. 7:30

2. What time does the clock show?
    A. 4:00
    B. 6:00
    Ⓒ 3:30
    D. 9:30

6. Ken wants to buy an ice cream cone for 75¢, a bag of potato chips for 50¢, and a drink for 95¢. How much money does he need?
    A. $3.00   B. $2.23   Ⓒ $2.20   D. $1.95

3. What time does the clock show?
    A. 10:05
    Ⓑ 8:15
    C. 8:03
    D. 8:30

7. Keisha spent $1.35 at the school store. How much change did she get from $2.00?
    Ⓐ 65¢   B. 75¢   C. 60¢   D. 95¢

8. Nate looked under the cushion of the couch and found some change. He found 1 quarter, 3 dimes, 2 nickels, and 7 pennies. How much money did he find?
    A. $1.35   B. $2.04   C. $0.98   Ⓓ $0.72

4. If the clock shows the time right now, what time will it be one hour from now?
    A. 9:00
    B. 10:00
    Ⓒ 7:00
    D. 12:00

9. Kaitlin has saved $18.25 to buy a birthday gift for her mother. She wants to buy her some perfume that costs $25.00. How much more money does Kaitlin need to save before she can buy the perfume?
    A. $7.00   B. $5.00   C. $6.25   Ⓓ $6.75

Total Problems: ___ Total Correct: ___ Score: ___   ⑦
© Carson-Dellosa CD-2210

Name _____   **Place Value**

Study the example below. Write the value of each underlined digit on the line provided.

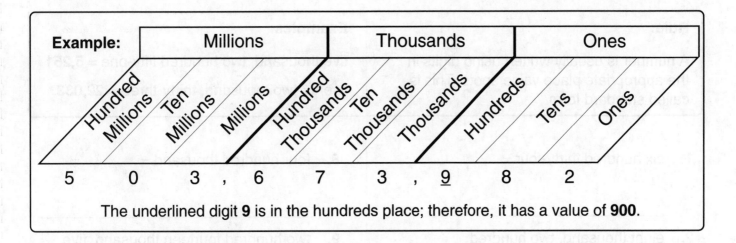

| Example: | Millions | | | Thousands | | | Ones | | |

The underlined digit **9** is in the hundreds place; therefore, it has a value of **900**.

1. 6<u>8</u>

Ten

2. 20<u>3</u>

ones

3. <u>3</u>56

hundred

4. 27<u>8</u>

ones

5. 4<u>5</u>6

tens

6. 2,<u>3</u>48

hundreds

7. <u>4</u>,438

Thousands

8. <u>3</u>7,894

Ten thousands

9. 62,<u>8</u>05

hundred

10. <u>9</u>42,018

hundred thousands

11. 16<u>4</u>,388

thousands

12. 2<u>3</u>6,195

hundred thousands

13. 687,<u>3</u>20

hundred

14. <u>5</u>,941,603

Millions

15. 7,<u>4</u>38,821

hundred thousands

| Total Problems: | Total Correct: | Score: |

Study the box below. Then, write each number in standard numerical form on the line provided.

Rule:	Examples:
A number is usually written using digits in the appropriate place value spots. This is called standard form.	five thousand, two hundred fifty-one = **5,251** twenty-two thousand, thirty-three = **22,033**

1. six hundred thirty-four =

_____

2. eight thousand, two hundred fifty-one =

_____

3. nine thousand, three hundred twenty-two =

_____

4. twenty-seven thousand, eight hundred =

_____

5. seventy thousand, one hundred two =

_____

6. eighty-three thousand, three hundred eleven =

_____

7. seven hundred eighty-two thousand, sixteen =

_____

8. four hundred thousand =

_____

9. two hundred fourteen thousand, five hundred three =

_____

10. nine hundred eight thousand, five hundred two =

_____

11. sixty one thousand, five =

_____

12. one hundred forty thousand, fifteen =

_____

13. eighty-one thousand, three hundred twelve =

_____

14. seven thousand, ninety =

_____

Total Problems: _____ Total Correct: _____ Score: _____

Study the box below. For each problem, circle the letter beside the correct answer.

Rule:	Examples:
Expanded notation is writing a number to show the value of each digit in the number.	583 = **500 + 80 + 3** Six hundred fifty-two = **600 + 50 + 2**

1. Eight hundred seventy-five =

    A. 8,000 + 75

    B. 800 + 75

    C. 80,000 + 700 + 50

    D. 800,000 + 75

4. 700 + 30 + 6 =

    A. 17,360

    B. 7,063

    C. 736

    D. 7,036

2. Six thousand, forty-eight =

    A. 6,000 + 400 + 80

    B. 10,000 + 6,000 + 400 + 80

    C. 6,000 + 40 + 8

    D. 60,000 + 40 + 8

5. 9,000 + 400 + 20 + 8 =

    A. 928

    B. 9,128

    C. 94,208

    D. 9,428

3. Eighteen thousand, five hundred seven =

    A. 10,000 + 8,000 + 500 + 7

    B. 1,000 + 800 + 20 + 7

    C. 10,000 + 8,000 + 500 + 70

    D. 10,000 + 50 + 7

6. 50,000 + 9,000 + 600 + 40 + 1 =

    A. 5,964

    B. 59,641

    C. 596,401

    D. 802,135

Total Problems:	Total Correct:	Score:

Study the examples below. To compare each pair of numbers, use less than (<), greater than (>), or equal to (=). Place the symbol in the square provided.

> **Examples:** 375 $\boxed{<}$ 475   7,000 $\boxed{=}$ 7,000   3,482 $\boxed{>}$ 2,843

1.	620 $\square$ 6,200		**4.**	9,286 $\square$ 13,489		**7.**	45,015 $\square$ 45,016	
2.	493 $\square$ 439		**5.**	724 $\square$ 724		**8.**	397,124 $\square$ 387,425	
3.	6,432 $\square$ 16,408		**6.**	3,080 $\square$ 3,800		**9.**	488,188 $\square$ 488,018	

Study the example below. On the line provided, order each set of numbers from least to greatest.

> **Example:**
>
> The series 235, 462, 183 would be properly ordered as **183, 235, 462**.

10. 43, 28, 17

_____

11. 623, 185, 94

_____

12. 613, 419, 582

_____

13. 101, 110, 210, 109

_____

14. 751, 739, 839, 749

_____

15. 450, 449, 339, 180

_____

16. 4,810; 6,412; 3,789; 6,413

_____

17. 5,725; 7,415; 4,535; 6,845

_____

Total Problems: _____ **Total Correct:** _____ **Score:** _____

Study the box below. Round each number to the nearest 10. Then, write the answer on the line provided.

Rule:	Examples:
Round numbers to the nearest 10 by checking the digit in the ones place value spot.	43 rounds to **40**
	68 rounds to **70**
If that digit is 5 or greater, round up to the next 10. If it is 4 or lower, keep the same 10 and change the ones digit to a 0.	439 rounds to **440**

1. 46 rounds to _____

2. 338 rounds to _____

3. 84 rounds to _____

4. 32 rounds to _____

5. 235 rounds to _____

6. 168 rounds to _____

7. 349 rounds to _____

8. 1,475 rounds to _____

9. 3,188 rounds to _____

10. 2,081 rounds to _____

11. 4,111 rounds to _____

12. 6,285 rounds to _____

13. 8,522 rounds to _____

14. 5,477 rounds to _____

15. 7,284 rounds to _____

16. 9,666 rounds to _____

Total Problems:	Total Correct:	Score:

Name _____

Study the box below. Round each number to the nearest 100. Then, write the answer on the line provided.

Rule:	Examples:
Round numbers to the nearest 100 by checking the digit in the tens place value spot.	132 rounds to **100**
If that digit is 5 or greater, round up to the next 100. If it is 4 or lower, keep the same 100. Remember to change the ones and tens digits to 0.	364 rounds to **400**
	5,682 rounds to **5,700**

1. 284 rounds to _____

2. 443 rounds to _____

3. 538 rounds to _____

4. 651 rounds to _____

5. 894 rounds to _____

6. 777 rounds to _____

7. 326 rounds to _____

8. 527 rounds to _____

9. 152 rounds to _____

10. 1,324 rounds to _____

11. 2,861 rounds to _____

12. 1,555 rounds to _____

13. 4,506 rounds to _____

14. 3,250 rounds to _____

15. 6,875 rounds to _____

16. 9,256 rounds to _____

Total Problems:	Total Correct:	Score:

Solve the word problems. Show your work and write the answers in the space provided.

417) 400) 390) 388

1. Write the number that has a 7 in the hundreds place, a 9 in the tens place, and a 4 in the ones place.

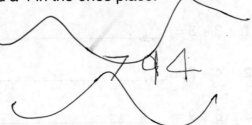

2. Show the number 4,562 in expanded notation.

3. Write the number 600 + 80 + 5 in standard form.

4. Doug has 76 marbles. Rounded to the nearest 10, about how many marbles does he have?

5. List 4 numbers that come between 352 and 421.

6. Write 6 numbers in order from least to greatest that are higher than 1,234.

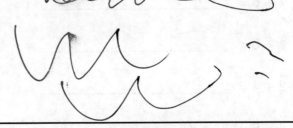

7. Jarron has 2 birds, 1 cat, and 2 dogs. How many animals have fur?

8. Theresa won 4 tokens at the arcade. The toy she wants requires 3 tokens. Can she get the toy?

Total Problems: **Total Correct:**   **Score:**

100% ✓

Add. Then, write the answer on the line provided.

1. 5 + 2 = _____ 7

2. 3 + 6 = _____ 9

3. 4 + 9 = _____ 13

4. 7 + 5 = _____ 12

5. 8 + 3 = _____ 11

6. 2 + 9 = _____ 11

7. 7 + 8 = _____ 15

8. 1 + 6 = _____ 7

9. 2 + 4 = _____ 6

10. 4 + 5 = _____ 9

11. 10 + 7 = _____ 17

12. 2 + 11 = _____ 13

13. 8 + 4 = _____ 12

14. 6 + 5 = _____ 11

15. 7 + 6 = _____ 13

16. 5 + 11 = _____ 16

17. 1 + 12 = _____ 13

18. 9 + 7 = _____ 16

19. 8 + 5 = _____ 13

20. 2 + 6 = _____ 8

21. 3 + 3 = _____ 6

22. 4 + 7 = _____ 11

23. 8 + 9 = _____ 17

24. 10 + 3 = _____ 13

25. 6 + 8 = _____ 14

26. 2 + 3 = _____ 5

27. 8 + 10 = _____ 18

28. 11 + 3 = _____ 14

29. 10 + 10 = _____ 20

30. 3 + 9 = _____ 12

31. 7 + 7 = _____ 14

32. 9 + 6 = _____ 15

33. 12 + 4 = _____ 16

34. 11 + 9 = _____ 20

35. 5 + 11 = _____ 16

36. 12 + 12 = _____ 24

16

| Total Problems: | Total Correct: | Score: |

Study the box below. Solve each problem and write the answer in the space provided.

Rule:
1. Add the ones column.
2. Add the tens column.
3. Add the hundreds column.
4. Continue to add columns as needed.

Example:

```
  132,378        132,378        132,378        132,378        132,378        132,378
+ 521,421      + 521,421      + 521,421      + 521,421      + 521,421      + 521,421
        9             99            799          3,799         53,799        653,799
```

1.	15 + 4 *19*	**6.**	54 + 14	**11.**	334 + 252	**16.**	3,296 + 2,703

1. 15
  + 4
  19

2. 24
  + 4
  28

3. 30
  + 12

4. 26
  + 21

5. 32
  + 25

6. 54
  + 14

7. 62
  + 15

8. 84
  + 13

9. 134
  + 53

10. 462
  + 125

11. 334
  + 252

12. 641
  + 227

13. 2,413
  + 1,352

14. 2,461
  + 3,425

15. 7,849
  + 2,140

16. 3,296
  + 2,703

17. 42,334
  + 31,360

18. 75,214
  + 13,662

19. 290,431
  + 307,553

20. 216,378
  + 521,421

Total Problems: **Total Correct:**   **Score:**

Name _____

Study the box below. Solve each problem and write the answer in the space provided.

Rule:

1. Add the ones column, then regroup.
2. Add the tens column, then regroup.
3. Add the hundreds column, then regroup.
4. Continue to add columns and regroup as needed.

Example:

$$
\begin{array}{r} 21\,7{,}38\overset{1}{8} \\ +\,69\,2{,}438 \\ \hline 6 \end{array}
\qquad
\begin{array}{r} 21\,7{,}\overset{1}{3}\overset{1}{8}8 \\ +\,69\,2{,}438 \\ \hline 26 \end{array}
\qquad
\begin{array}{r} 21\,7{,}\overset{1}{3}8\overset{1}{8} \\ +\,69\,2{,}438 \\ \hline 826 \end{array}
\qquad
\begin{array}{r} 21\,\overset{1}{7}{,}\overset{1}{3}88 \\ +\,69\,2{,}438 \\ \hline 9{,}826 \end{array}
\qquad
\begin{array}{r} 2\overset{1}{1}\,7{,}\overset{1}{3}88 \\ +\,69\,2{,}438 \\ \hline 09{,}826 \end{array}
\qquad
\begin{array}{r} \overset{1}{2}1\,7{,}\overset{1}{3}\overset{1}{8}8 \\ +\,69\,2{,}438 \\ \hline 909{,}826 \end{array}
$$

1. $\begin{array}{r}35\\+\,27\\\hline\end{array}$	**6.** $\begin{array}{r}85\\+\,56\\\hline\end{array}$	**11.** $\begin{array}{r}348\\+\,235\\\hline\end{array}$	**16.** $\begin{array}{r}628\\+\,597\\\hline\end{array}$
2. $\begin{array}{r}28\\+\,14\\\hline\end{array}$	**7.** $\begin{array}{r}78\\+\,66\\\hline\end{array}$	**12.** $\begin{array}{r}565\\+\,217\\\hline\end{array}$	**17.** $\begin{array}{r}4{,}188\\+\,176\\\hline\end{array}$
3. $\begin{array}{r}62\\+\,39\\\hline\end{array}$	**8.** $\begin{array}{r}97\\+\,45\\\hline\end{array}$	**13.** $\begin{array}{r}757\\+\,386\\\hline\end{array}$	**18.** $\begin{array}{r}5{,}264\\+\,6{,}478\\\hline\end{array}$
4. $\begin{array}{r}72\\+\,49\\\hline\end{array}$	**9.** $\begin{array}{r}68\\+\,77\\\hline\end{array}$	**14.** $\begin{array}{r}898\\+\,467\\\hline\end{array}$	**19.** $\begin{array}{r}2{,}357\\+\,4{,}991\\\hline\end{array}$
5. $\begin{array}{r}55\\+\,67\\\hline\end{array}$	**10.** $\begin{array}{r}239\\+\,164\\\hline\end{array}$	**15.** $\begin{array}{r}954\\+\,375\\\hline\end{array}$	**20.** $\begin{array}{r}37{,}835\\+\,24{,}638\\\hline\end{array}$

Total Problems: _____ **Total Correct:** _____ **Score:** _____

Read the box below. Solve each problem. Then, write the answer in the space provided.

Tip: Keep the place values lined up properly to be sure you find the right sum.

1.   62
   + 43

2.   75
   + 85

3.   54
   + 92

4.   726
   + 685

5.   201
    436
    313
   + 542

6.   736
     89
   + 104

7. 3,482
    437
   + 68

8. 246
   442
   + 53

9. 462
   129
   + 513

10. 315
   127
   382
   + 98

11. 6,428
   1,375
   + 3,684

12. 30,147
   25,236
   + 42,613

13. 2,804
   1,366
   + 5,391

14. 16,284
   2,590
   + 177

15. 623
   431
   907
   + 75

16. 5,894
   1,388
   + 3,137

17. 28,123
   33,294
   + 46,510

18. 14,738
   22,856
   + 17,979

19. 30,164
   23,606
   + 48,224

20. 1,425
   4,138
    621
   + 521

Total Problems: _____ **Total Correct:** _____ **Score:** _____

Study the examples below. Round each number to the greatest place value position. Then, write the answer on the line provided.

> **Examples:**
> 25 rounds to **30**
> 473 rounds to **500**

1. 27 rounds to _____

2. 83 rounds to _____

3. 35 rounds to _____

4. 72 rounds to _____

5. 80 rounds to _____

6. 96 rounds to _____

7. 94 rounds to _____

8. 18 rounds to _____

9. 356 rounds to _____

10. 782 rounds to _____

11. 372 rounds to _____

12. 935 rounds to _____

Using the space to the right of each problem, round both numbers. Then, estimate each sum and write the answer in the space provided.

13.   23
    + 19

14.   34
    + 86

15.   45
    + 23

16.   97
    + 38

17. 124
    + 173

18. 365
    + 284

19.   419
    + 477

20.   946
    + 817

21. 4,284
    + 6,746

22.   9,378
    + 2,481

23.   6,089
    + 2,784

24.   3,496
    + 578

20

| Total Problems: | Total Correct: | Score: |

Using the space to the right of each problem, round both numbers. Then, estimate each sum and write the answer in the space provided.

1.	82 + 98	**7.**	575 + 185	**13.**	987 + 479	**19.**	7,252 + 2,781
2.	51 + 74	**8.**	618 + 537	**14.**	2,408 + 1,375	**20.**	8,517 + 5,670
3.	28 + 65	**9.**	386 + 257	**15.**	3,993 + 5,651	**21.**	38,974 + 25,162
4.	41 + 52	**10.**	411 + 353	**16.**	4,197 + 8,214	**22.**	53,794 + 52,759
5.	486 + 178	**11.**	914 + 807	**17.**	5,312 + 4,960	**23.**	47,997 + 41,258
6.	839 + 354	**12.**	752 + 693	**18.**	6,153 + 3,821	**24.**	63,983 + 29,171

Solve the word problems. Show your work and write the answers in the space provided.

1. Andre collected 19 rocks on the first day of the hike. On the second day, he collected 23. On the third day, he found 14 more. How many did he collect in all?

4. Nadine drove 284 miles one day and 374 the next. Estimate how many miles she drove in all.

2. Robin sold 145 bars of candy the first week of the fund-raiser. The second week she sold 207. How many candy bars did she sell in all?

5. Keela saw 325 different cars on Friday and 287 different cars on Saturday. How many different cars did she see in all?

3. During April, Juanita sold fresh flowers at her mother's flower stand. She sold 31 dozen flowers the first week, 27 dozen the second week, 19 dozen the third week, and 14 dozen the fourth week. How many dozens of flowers did she sell during April?

6. Kalon picked 1,486 strawberries at his grandparents' farm one week. He picked 288 strawberries each week for two more weeks. How many did he pick in all?

Total Problems: _____   Total Correct: _____   Score: _____

Name _____

Subtract. Write the answers on the lines provided.

1. 8 – 6 = __2__

2. 10 – 8 = __2__

3. 7 – 4 = __3__

4. 9 – 3 = __6__

5. 8 – 3 = __5__

6. 6 – 3 = __3__

7. 3 – 1 = __2__

8. 4 – 3 = __1__

9. 11 – 5 = __6__

10. 12 – 6 = __6__

11. 16 – 8 = __8__

12. 13 – 6 = __7__

13. 15 – 5 = __10__

14. 14 – 8 = __6__

15. 9 – 6 = __3__

16. 18 – 9 = __9__

17. 17 – 8 = __9__

18. 14 – 9 = __5__

19. 20 – 10 = __10__

20. 14 – 6 = __8__

21. 18 – 7 = __9__

22. 16 – 6 = __10__

23. 10 – 5 = __5__

24. 12 – 2 = __10__

25. 10 – 3 = __7__

26. 20 – 11 = __9__

27. 17 – 5 = __12__

28. 18 – 6 = __12__

29. 14 – 7 = __7__

30. 11 – 2 = __9__

31. 8 – 4 = __4__

32. 12 – 4 = __8__

33. 13 – 9 = __4__

34. 17 – 7 = __10__

35. 21 – 11 = __10__

36. 24 – 12 = __12__

Total Problems: 36   **Total Correct:** 36   **Score:** 36

Study the box below. Subtract each problem without regrouping. Then, write the answer in the space provided.

Rule:

1. Subtract the ones column.
2. Subtract the tens column.
3. Subtract the hundreds column.
4. Continue to subtract each column as needed.

Example:

```
  9 8,2 7|3|        9 8,2|7|3         9 8,2 7 3        9|8,2 7 3        |9 8,2 7 3
− 5 1,1 5|2|      − 5 1,1|5|2       − 5 1,1 5 2      − 5|1,1 5 2       |− 5 1,1 5 2
         |1|             |2|1             1 2 1          7,1 2 1         4 7,1 2 1
```

1.	17 − 6	6.	46 − 25	11.	84 − 53	16.	478 − 316
2.	15 − 4	7.	27 − 13	12.	75 − 31	17.	2,568 − 354
3.	23 − 12	8.	42 − 31	13.	124 − 113	18.	4,782 − 1,371
4.	17 − 10	9.	55 − 23	14.	342 − 231	19.	2,807 − 1,500
5.	38 − 24	10.	67 − 36	15.	794 − 562	20.	9,487 − 6,235

Total Problems: _____   Total Correct: _____   Score: _____

Study the box below. Solve each problem using regrouping. Then, write the answer in the space provided.

Rule:

1. Regroup, then subtract the ones column.
2. Regroup, then subtract the tens column.
3. Regroup, then subtract the hundreds column.
4. Continue to subtract columns and regroup as needed.
5. When you regroup, the number to the left is decreased by one.

Example:

$$
\begin{array}{r}
342,5\overset{2\ 15}{3}5 \\
147,079 \\
\hline
6
\end{array}
\qquad
\begin{array}{r}
342,\overset{4\ 12\ 15}{5}35 \\
-147,079 \\
\hline
56
\end{array}
\qquad
\begin{array}{r}
342,\overset{4\ 12\ 15}{5}35 \\
-147,079 \\
\hline
456
\end{array}
\qquad
\begin{array}{r}
34\overset{3\ 12\ 4\ 12\ 15}{2},535 \\
-147,079 \\
\hline
5,456
\end{array}
\qquad
\begin{array}{r}
3\overset{2\ 13\ 12\ 4\ 12\ 15}{4}2,535 \\
-147,079 \\
\hline
95,456
\end{array}
\qquad
\begin{array}{r}
\overset{2\ 13\ 12\ 4\ 12\ 15}{3}42,535 \\
-147,079 \\
\hline
195,456
\end{array}
$$

1.	52 − 39	**6.**	980 − 430	**11.**	7,303 − 3,855	**16.**	49,718 − 32,579
2.	47 − 19	**7.**	543 − 298	**12.**	8,624 − 4,937	**17.**	38,972 − 24,687
3.	61 − 25	**8.**	766 − 384	**13.**	5,322 − 1,404	**18.**	15,476 − 13,287
4.	312 − 105	**9.**	781 − 366	**14.**	7,362 − 4,564	**19.**	65,980 − 31,799
5.	614 − 256	**10.**	4,901 − 2,875	**15.**	82,712 − 69,934	**20.**	49,718 − 32,579

Total Problems: **Total Correct:**   **Score:**

Name _____

Study the box below. Subtract and write the answer in the space provided.

Rule:	Example:
Begin subtracting in the ones place value position. When there are not enough ones from which to subtract, regroup tens. When there are not enough tens, regroup hundreds, and so on, as needed.	1 9 10 2̸ 0̸ 0̸ − 3 4 ――――― 1 6 6

1.   40
   − 19

2.   30
   − 15

3.   70
   − 24

4.   150
   − 36

5.   250
   − 33

6.   200
   − 165

7.   270
   − 136

8.   400
   − 320

9.   300
   − 134

10.   800
    − 522

11.   500
    − 278

12.   700
    − 484

13.   1,000
    − 256

14.   2,500
    − 1,387

15.   7,000
    − 3,572

16.   6,000
    − 4,829

17.   4,500
    − 3,271

18.   9,000
    − 7,358

19.   10,000
    − 8,462

20.   10,000
    − 9,897

Total Problems: _____   Total Correct: _____   Score: _____

Name _____

Answer each problem in the space provided. Use regrouping as needed.

1. 496 − 237	**7.** 1,800 − 539	**13.** 79,136 − 5,564	**19.** 300,000 − 273,189
2. 742 − 429	**8.** 28,362 − 14,795	**14.** 97,612 − 46,378	**20.** 465,238 − 254,189
3. 643 − 286	**9.** 34,607 − 25,350	**15.** 42,320 − 41,412	**21.** 489,284 − 232,422
4. 828 − 537	**10.** 24,816 − 18,912	**16.** 88,177 − 66,250	**22.** 1,777,333 − 455,999
5. 726 − 618	**11.** 45,324 − 41,188	**17.** 120,436 − 75,328	**23.** 906,589 − 552,978
6. 1,398 − 852	**12.** 50,000 − 31,217	**18.** 250,000 − 175,000	**24.** 2,001,551 − 987,845

Total Problems: **Total Correct:**   **Score:**

Answer each problem in the space provided.

1. $\begin{array}{r} 35 \\ -\ 9 \\ \hline \end{array}$	**8.** $\begin{array}{r} 700 \\ -522 \\ \hline \end{array}$	**15.** $\begin{array}{r} 96{,}132 \\ -\ 37{,}488 \\ \hline \end{array}$	**22.** $\begin{array}{r} 305{,}061 \\ -\ 184{,}235 \\ \hline \end{array}$
2. $\begin{array}{r} 72 \\ -40 \\ \hline \end{array}$	**9.** $\begin{array}{r} 350 \\ -207 \\ \hline \end{array}$	**16.** $\begin{array}{r} 93{,}246 \\ -\ 75{,}369 \\ \hline \end{array}$	**23.** $\begin{array}{r} 704{,}188 \\ -\ 96{,}256 \\ \hline \end{array}$
3. $\begin{array}{r} 184 \\ -\ 69 \\ \hline \end{array}$	**10.** $\begin{array}{r} 7{,}521 \\ -\ 3{,}488 \\ \hline \end{array}$	**17.** $\begin{array}{r} 100{,}000 \\ -\ 54{,}000 \\ \hline \end{array}$	**24.** $\begin{array}{r} 846{,}137 \\ -\ 278{,}429 \\ \hline \end{array}$
4. $\begin{array}{r} 136 \\ -\ 78 \\ \hline \end{array}$	**11.** $\begin{array}{r} 10{,}892 \\ -\ 7{,}468 \\ \hline \end{array}$	**18.** $\begin{array}{r} 105{,}111 \\ -\ 63{,}999 \\ \hline \end{array}$	**25.** $\begin{array}{r} 600{,}000 \\ -\ 159{,}744 \\ \hline \end{array}$
5. $\begin{array}{r} 257 \\ -\ 34 \\ \hline \end{array}$	**12.** $\begin{array}{r} 9{,}464 \\ -\ 3{,}597 \\ \hline \end{array}$	**19.** $\begin{array}{r} 122{,}555 \\ -\ 77{,}878 \\ \hline \end{array}$	**26.** $\begin{array}{r} 940{,}905 \\ -\ 88{,}499 \\ \hline \end{array}$
6. $\begin{array}{r} 521 \\ -356 \\ \hline \end{array}$	**13.** $\begin{array}{r} 43{,}282 \\ -\ 31{,}465 \\ \hline \end{array}$	**20.** $\begin{array}{r} 155{,}232 \\ -\ 86{,}456 \\ \hline \end{array}$	**27.** $\begin{array}{r} 1{,}300{,}588 \\ -\ 455{,}297 \\ \hline \end{array}$
7. $\begin{array}{r} 688 \\ -309 \\ \hline \end{array}$	**14.** $\begin{array}{r} 85{,}016 \\ -\ 54{,}258 \\ \hline \end{array}$	**21.** $\begin{array}{r} 200{,}000 \\ -\ 86{,}555 \\ \hline \end{array}$	**28.** $\begin{array}{r} 1{,}566{,}892 \\ -\ 578{,}489 \\ \hline \end{array}$

Total Problems: **Total Correct:**   **Score:**

Solve the word problems. Show your work and write the answers in the space provided.

1. Delaney had 27 days to work on her science project. After working for 13 days, she was half finished. How many days did she have left to work on her project?

5. Tara's mother baked 72 chocolate chip cookies and 145 sugar cookies. If 89 sugar cookies were eaten, how many sugar cookies remained?

2. Isaiah's father took a trip that was 396 miles long. He drove 115 miles the first day. How many miles did he have left to drive?

6. Zachary's basketball team scored 800 points in their second season. In their first season, they scored 650 points. How many more points did they score in the second season?

3. The pet store had 648 goldfish. Employees sold 394 goldfish in one week. How many goldfish were left?

7. Mr. Fleming's copier made 45,862 copies in July. In August, the copier made 65,012 copies. How many more copies did it make in August?

4. Margaret collected 1,498 stickers. She gave 745 to her friends. How many did she have left?

8. Antoine rode his bike 372 miles in May. In June he rode 224 miles. How many more miles did he ride in May?

Total Problems: _____   Total Correct: _____   Score: _____

Name _____

Study the box below. Then, answer each problem on the line provided.

Rule: 0 multiplied by any number will always equal 0. Any number multiplied by 1 will always equal that number.	**Examples:** 0 x 5 = **0** 5 x 1 = **5** 0 x 10 = **0** 12 x 1 = **12** 0 x 100 = **0** 100 x 1 = **100**

1. 0 x 2 = _____

2. 4 x 8 = _____

3. 2 x 2 = _____

4. 3 x 4 = _____

5. 2 x 1 = _____

6. 5 x 2 = _____

7. 3 x 3 = _____

8. 2 x 6 = _____

9. 5 x 8 = _____

10. 4 x 6 = _____

11. 5 x 3 = _____

12. 3 x 8 = _____

13. 3 x 7 = _____

14. 5 x 6 = _____

15. 2 x 9 = _____

16. 1 x 9 = _____

17. 4 x 12 = _____

18. 2 x 8 = _____

19. 3 x 10 = _____

20. 2 x 12 = _____

21. 0 x 4 = _____

22. 5 x 5 = _____

23. 2 x 10 = _____

24. 5 x 1 = _____

25. 3 x 9 = _____

26. 4 x 7 = _____

27. 3 x 2 = _____

28. 1 x 8 = _____

29. 0 x 3 = _____

30. 5 x 9 = _____

Total Problems: _____ **Total Correct:** _____ **Score:** _____

Study the box below. Then, solve the problems and write each answer on the line provided.

Rule: Multiplying is just a faster way of adding. By learning the basic facts, you can find out "how many in all" much faster.	**Example:** 3 x 6 = ___ 3 x 6 = 3 groups of 6 things, like books 6 books + 6 books + 6 books = **18** books 3 x 6 = **18**

1. 6 x 4 = _____

2. 8 x 5 = _____

3. 7 x 3 = _____

4. 8 x 8 = _____

5. 9 x 7 = _____

6. 7 x 8 = _____

7. 6 x 8 = _____

8. 7 x 10 = _____

9. 6 x 5 = _____

10. 9 x 9 = _____

11. 8 x 10 = _____

12. 8 x 4 = _____

13. 7 x 5 = _____

14. 9 x 8 = _____

15. 6 x 2 = _____

16. 8 x 6 = _____

17. 9 x 2 = _____

18. 9 x 11 = _____

19. 6 x 12 = _____

20. 9 x 3 = _____

21. 6 x 9 = _____

22. 9 x 4 = _____

23. 7 x 6 = _____

24. 7 x 9 = _____

25. 6 x 10 = _____

26. 9 x 5 = _____

27. 6 x 6 = _____

28. 7 x 7 = _____

29. 9 x 12 = _____

30. 6 x 7 = _____

Total Problems: _____   **Total Correct:** _____   **Score:** _____

Name _____

Multiply each problem. Then, write the answer in the space provided.

1. 1 x 6	**9.** 5 x 5	**17.** 5 x 2	**25.** 10 x 3
2. 3 x 7	**10.** 6 x 5	**18.** 9 x 3	**26.** 4 x 9
3. 4 x 5	**11.** 9 x 2	**19.** 12 x 2	**27.** 11 x 4
4. 6 x 4	**12.** 3 x 3	**20.** 12 x 3	**28.** 10 x 4
5. 3 x 8	**13.** 9 x 5	**21.** 8 x 9	**29.** 10 x 5
6. 2 x 7	**14.** 8 x 7	**22.** 5 x 7	**30.** 11 x 7
7. 8 x 6	**15.** 12 x 8	**23.** 11 x 5	**31.** 12 x 9
8. 4 x 3	**16.** 10 x 7	**24.** 11 x 9	**32.** 11 x 8

Total Problems: **Total Correct:**   **Score:**

Name _____

Study the box below. Then, solve each problem. Write the answer in the space provided.

Rule:	Example:
Multiply ones, then regroup.	$\overset{1}{23}$ $\qquad$ $\overset{1}{23}$
Multiply tens, then add extra tens.	$\underline{\times\ 6}$ $\qquad$ $\underline{\times\ 6}$
	$\qquad$ 8 $\qquad\quad$ 138

1. $\quad$ 10
$\underline{\times\ 5}$

2. $\quad$ 10
$\underline{\times\ 3}$

3. $\quad$ 12
$\underline{\times\ 2}$

4. $\quad$ 11
$\underline{\times\ 3}$

5. $\quad$ 13
$\underline{\times\ 5}$

6. $\quad$ 10
$\underline{\times\ 4}$

7. $\quad$ 15
$\underline{\times\ 4}$

8. $\quad$ 19
$\underline{\times\ 2}$

9. $\quad$ 31
$\underline{\times\ 4}$

10. $\quad$ 48
$\underline{\times\ 3}$

11. $\quad$ 30
$\underline{\times\ 6}$

12. $\quad$ 24
$\underline{\times\ 5}$

13. $\quad$ 62
$\underline{\times\ 2}$

14. $\quad$ 27
$\underline{\times\ 3}$

15. $\quad$ 54
$\underline{\times\ 3}$

16. $\quad$ 73
$\underline{\times\ 3}$

17. $\quad$ 97
$\underline{\times\ 3}$

18. $\quad$ 80
$\underline{\times\ 4}$

19. $\quad$ 79
$\underline{\times\ 3}$

20. $\quad$ 87
$\underline{\times\ 5}$

21. $\quad$ 90
$\underline{\times\ 4}$

22. $\quad$ 82
$\underline{\times\ 9}$

23. $\quad$ 94
$\underline{\times\ 7}$

24. $\quad$ 98
$\underline{\times\ 6}$

Study the box below. Then, solve each problem. Write the answer in the space provided.

Rule:	Example:
1. Multiply ones, then regroup.	423 423 423
2. Multiply tens, then add extra tens.	x 2 x 2 x 2
3. Multiply hundreds.	**6** **46** **846**
4. Regroup as needed.	

1. 100
    x 3

2. 120
    x 2

3. 300
    x 5

4. 250
    x 4

5. 145
    x 2

6. 278
    x 4

7. 329
    x 3

8. 640
    x 5

9. 710
    x 6

10. 518
    x 7

11. 422
    x 5

12. 705
    x 4

13. 826
    x 8

14. 900
    x 3

15. 715
    x 6

16. 827
    x 9

17. 926
    x 7

18. 686
    x 8

19. 912
    x 3

20. 847
    x 5

Total Problems: Total Correct: Score:

Name _____

Study the box below. Then, solve each problem. Write the answer in the space provided.

Rule:
1. Multiply ones by ones, tens, and hundreds. Regroup as needed.
2. Multiply tens by ones, tens, and hundreds. Regroup as needed.
3. Line up the second number under the tens place of the first number.
4. Add the two numbers to find the final product.

Example:

```
  325        325          325
x  43      x  43        x  43
 975        975          975
           1,300       +1,300
                       13,975
```

---

1.   203
        x 12

4.   330
        x 25

7.   633
        x 61

10.   567
        x 38

2.   370
        x 15

5.   451
        x 36

8.   357
        x 51

11.   629
        x 88

3.   150
        x 21

6.   522
        x 40

9.   278
        x 55

12.   783
        x 52

Total Problems: **Total Correct:**   **Score:**

Name _____

Study the box below. Round the two-digit factor and leave the one-digit factor as is. Multiply to find the estimated product. Then, write the answer in the space provided.

Rule:	**Example:**
Since it is easier to multiply by numbers ending in 0, it can be useful to estimate an approximate answer by rounding.	26 x 9 = _____ 26 rounds up to **30**, so the estimated product is: 30 x 9 = **270**

1.   18
    x 2

2.   23
    x 5

3.   15
    x 3

4.   33
    x 6

5.   46
    x 4

6.   24
    x 9

7.   58
    x 5

8.   64
    x 7

9.   72
    x 2

10.   53
    x 6

11.   75
    x 4

12.   81
    x 8

13.   94
    x 5

14.   70
    x 3

15.   98
    x 6

Total Problems: **Total Correct:**   **Score:**

Study the examples below. Round each factor to the greatest place value represented. Then, multiply to find the estimated product. Write the answer in the space provided.

Examples:

325	rounds to	300		5,928	rounds to	6,000
x 29	rounds to	x 30		x 12	rounds to	x 10
		9,000				**60,000**

1. 24
   x 31

2. 37
   x 26

3. 50
   x 35

4. 78
   x 64

5. 89
   x 29

6. 134
   x 20

7. 188
   x 43

8. 205
   x 29

9. 278
   x 41

10. 327
   x 56

11. 415
   x 92

12. 675
   x 85

13. 563
   x 47

14. 917
   x 39

15. 1,000
   x 25

16. 1,254
   x 36

Solve the word problems. Show your work and write the answers in the space provided.

1. Sophia's Bakery sold 8 cakes each day for 21 days. How many cakes did the bakery sell in all?

5. Regina made 49 gift baskets each week for 5 weeks. Estimate how many gift baskets she made.

2. For 21 days of camp, Melanie collected 2 souvenirs each day. How many souvenirs did she collect in all?

6. Donna sold 136 bags of popcorn at the movie theater for 24 days. Estimate to find out about how many bags of popcorn Donna sold.

3. Matt planted 25 fruit trees each day for 18 days. How many fruit trees did he plant in all?

7. Jerome practiced with his soccer team 4 hours each day for 159 days. How many hours in all did Jerome practice?

4. Mr. Sanders ordered 56 boxes of videotapes for his store. Each box had 35 tapes. How many videotapes did he receive in all?

8. Christina has collected 156 unusual coins every year for 18 years. How many coins has she collected in all?

Total Problems: _____   Total Correct: _____   Score: _____

Name _____

Study the box below. Solve each problem. Then, write the answer on the line provided.

Rules:	Examples:
0 divided by any number will always equal 0.	$0 \div 5 = 0$
Any number divided by 1 will always equal that number.	$8 \div 1 = 8$

1. $0 \div 12 =$ ___0___

2. $5 \div 1 =$ ___5___

3. $4 \div 1 =$ ___4___

4. $11 \div 1 =$ ___11___

5. $9 \div 1 =$ ___9___

6. $0 \div 7 =$ ___0___

7. $6 \div 1 =$ ___6___

8. $8 \div 1 =$ ___8___

9. $0 \div 10 =$ _____

10. $0 \div 3 =$ _____

11. $0 \div 9 =$ _____

12. $7 \div 1 =$ _____

13. $1 \div 1 =$ _____

14. $0 \div 4 =$ _____

15. $2 \div 1 =$ _____

16. $12 \div 1 =$ _____

17. $3 \div 1 =$ ___3___

18. $0 \div 6 =$ ___0___

19. $0 \div 1 =$ ___0___

20. $0 \div 2 =$ ___0___

21. $0 \div 8 =$ ___0___

22. $10 \div 1 =$ ___10___

23. $0 \div 11 =$ ___0___

24. $0 \div 5 =$ ___0___

Total Problems:	Total Correct:	Score:

Name _____

Study the box below. Solve each problem. Then, write the answer on the line provided.

| **Rule:** 10 items placed in groups of 2 equals 5 groups. | **Example:** $10 \div 2 = 5$  |

1. $16 \div 2 =$ ___8___

2. $14 \div 2 =$ ___7___

3. $12 \div 4 =$ ___3___

4. $22 \div 2 =$ ___11___

5. $20 \div 4 =$ ___5___

6. $28 \div 4 =$ ___7___

7. $30 \div 3 =$ ___10___

8. $12 \div 2 =$ ___6___

9. $18 \div 3 =$ ___6___

10. $4 \div 2 =$ ___2___

11. $9 \div 3 =$ ___3___

12. $8 \div 2 =$ ___4___

13. $24 \div 2 =$ _____

14. $36 \div 3 =$ ___16___

15. $18 \div 2 =$ ___9___

16. $15 \div 3 =$ _____

17. $33 \div 3 =$ _____

18. $27 \div 3 =$ _____

19. $24 \div 4 =$ _____

20. $3 \div 3 =$ _____

21. $40 \div 4 =$ _____

22. $10 \div 2 =$ _____

23. $4 \div 4 =$ ___1___

24. $48 \div 4 =$ _____

25. $36 \div 4 =$ _____

26. $20 \div 2 =$ _____

27. $2 \div 2 =$ ___1___

28. $24 \div 3 =$ _____

29. $21 \div 3 =$ _____

30. $44 \div 4 =$ _____

31. $32 \div 4 =$ _____

32. $10 \div 2 =$ ___5___

33. $6 \div 3 =$ ___2___

Total Problems: **Total Correct:**   **Score:**

Name_____

Solve each problem. Then, write the answer on the line provided.

1. $30 \div 5 =$ _____

2. $12 \div 6 =$ _____

3. $40 \div 5 =$ _____

4. $18 \div 6 =$ _____

5. $42 \div 6 =$ _____

6. $35 \div 7 =$ _____

7. $48 \div 6 =$ _____

8. $20 \div 5 =$ _____

9. $56 \div 7 =$ _____

10. $54 \div 6 =$ _____

11. $15 \div 5 =$ _____

12. $28 \div 7 =$ _____

13. $70 \div 7 =$ _____

14. $63 \div 7 =$ _____

15. $7 \div 7 =$ _____

16. $36 \div 6 =$ _____

17. $55 \div 5 =$ _____

18. $45 \div 5 =$ _____

19. $49 \div 7 =$ _____

20. $60 \div 6 =$ _____

21. $25 \div 5 =$ _____

22. $60 \div 5 =$ _____

23. $77 \div 7 =$ _____

24. $14 \div 7 =$ _____

25. $10 \div 5 =$ _____

26. $84 \div 7 =$ _____

27. $66 \div 6 =$ _____

Total Problems: **Total Correct:**   **Score:**

Name _____

Solve each problem. Write the answer on the line provided.

1. $16 \div 8 =$ _____

2. $36 \div 9 =$ _____

3. $88 \div 8 =$ _____

4. $45 \div 9 =$ _____

5. $27 \div 9 =$ _____

6. $40 \div 8 =$ _____

7. $8 \div 8 =$ _____

8. $48 \div 8 =$ _____

9. $24 \div 8 =$ _____

10. $72 \div 9 =$ _____

11. $32 \div 8 =$ _____

12. $81 \div 9 =$ _____

13. $90 \div 9 =$ _____

14. $64 \div 8 =$ _____

15. $18 \div 9 =$ _____

16. $9 \div 9 =$ _____

17. $54 \div 9 =$ _____

18. $56 \div 8 =$ _____

19. $72 \div 8 =$ _____

20. $80 \div 8 =$ _____

21. $96 \div 8 =$ _____

22. $63 \div 9 =$ _____

23. $108 \div 9 =$ _____

24. $99 \div 9 =$ _____

Total Problems: _____ **Total Correct:** _____ **Score:** _____

Name _____

Study the example below. Solve each problem. Then, write the answer in the space provided.

Example:	Think:
$$6\overline{)30}$$ with 5 on top and -30, remainder 0	6 divides evenly into 30, leaving no remainder.

1. $5\overline{)30}$ 5. $7\overline{)14}$ 9. $4\overline{)28}$ 13. $3\overline{)24}$

2. $3\overline{)18}$ 6. $8\overline{)56}$ 10. $3\overline{)33}$ 14. $8\overline{)64}$

3. $8\overline{)8}$ 7. $6\overline{)36}$ 11. $2\overline{)8}$ 15. $9\overline{)81}$

4. $4\overline{)32}$ 8. $1\overline{)4}$ 12. $8\overline{)40}$ 16. $2\overline{)18}$

Total Problems: **Total Correct:**   **Score:**   43

Name _____

Study the example below. Then, solve each problem. Show your work and write the answer in the space provided.

Example:

$$\overset{12}{4\overline{)48}}$$
$$\underline{-4}$$
$$08$$
$$\underline{-8}$$
$$0$$

Think:

4 divides evenly into 48, leaving no remainder.

1. $2\overline{)64}$

2. $3\overline{)69}$

3. $4\overline{)32}$

4. $9\overline{)90}$

5. $3\overline{)36}$

6. $4\overline{)84}$

7. $6\overline{)72}$

8. $6\overline{)84}$

9. $2\overline{)98}$

10. $4\overline{)100}$

11. $5\overline{)125}$

12. $3\overline{)123}$

Total Problems: _____ Total Correct: _____ Score: _____

Study the example below. Then, solve each problem. Show your work and write the answer in the space provided.

Example:

$$8 \text{ R3}$$
$$4\overline{)35}$$
$$\underline{-32}$$
$$3$$

Think:

35 divided by 4 is **8** because 8 x 4 is closest to 35 without exceeding 35.

Then, 35 – 32 is 3, and **3** is called the remainder.

1. $4\overline{)75}$

5. $6\overline{)63}$

9. $9\overline{)98}$

13. $7\overline{)87}$

2. $3\overline{)52}$

6. $8\overline{)89}$

10. $3\overline{)34}$

14. $2\overline{)39}$

3. $5\overline{)57}$

7. $4\overline{)93}$

11. $4\overline{)65}$

15. $5\overline{)66}$

4. $2\overline{)47}$

8. $5\overline{)74}$

12. $3\overline{)54}$

16. $8\overline{)99}$

Study the example below. Then, estimate the quotient for each problem. Show your work and write the answer in the space provided.

Example:

$4\overline{)62}$

Round 62 to the nearest 10.

$4\overline{)60}$

Then, divide as usual.

$$\begin{array}{r} 15 \\ 4\overline{)60} \\ -4 \\ \hline 20 \\ -20 \\ \hline 0 \end{array}$$

Therefore, the estimated quotient is **15**.

1. $5\overline{)47}$

2. $3\overline{)27}$

3. $5\overline{)57}$

4. $2\overline{)47}$

5. $6\overline{)63}$

6. $9\overline{)89}$

7. $4\overline{)96}$

8. $5\overline{)74}$

9. $5\overline{)98}$

10. $3\overline{)34}$

11. $5\overline{)65}$

12. $3\overline{)58}$

46

Total Problems: _____   Total Correct: _____   Score: _____

Solve the word problems. Show your work and write the answers in the space provided.

1. Stan had 32 bags of popcorn to sell at the snack bar. He sold all of the popcorn to 8 customers. If each customer bought the same number of popcorn bags, how many bags did each buy?

4. Ms. Davis drove 325 miles in 5 days. If she drove the same number of miles each day, how many miles did she drive?

2. Phil sold 146 magazine subscriptions. He worked for 2 weeks and sold the same amount each week. How many subscriptions did he sell each week?

5. Reginald has 162 seeds to plant in his garden. If he digs 18 holes in the soil and distributes the seeds equally, how many seeds can he put in each hole?

3. Sue-Yin sold 48 pencils from her supply store. The pencils were wrapped to hold 6 in each set. How many sets did Sue-Yin sell?

6. Coretta bought 436 roses for the Mother's Day Banquet. She gave 2 roses to each mother at the banquet. If all of the roses were given away, how many mothers attended the banquet?

Total Problems: _____ Total Correct: _____ Score: _____

Study the example below. Circle the fraction which names the shaded part of each figure.

Example:

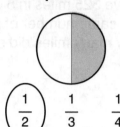

$\frac{1}{2}$ $\frac{1}{3}$ $\frac{1}{4}$

Think:

A fraction names a part of the whole. Since 1 out of 2 parts of the circle is shaded, $\frac{1}{2}$ names the shaded part.

1.

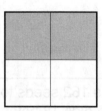

$\frac{2}{3}$ $\frac{2}{4}$ $\frac{2}{6}$

4.

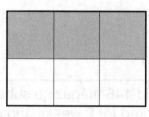

$\frac{2}{3}$ $\frac{3}{6}$ $\frac{4}{5}$

2.

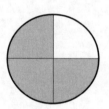

$\frac{2}{3}$ $\frac{3}{4}$ $\frac{4}{6}$

5.

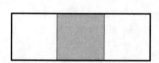

$\frac{1}{2}$ $\frac{1}{3}$ $\frac{1}{4}$

3.

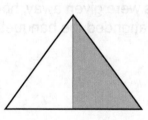

$\frac{1}{2}$ $\frac{1}{4}$ $\frac{1}{5}$

6.

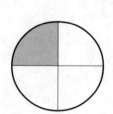

$\frac{1}{2}$ $\frac{1}{3}$ $\frac{1}{4}$

Total Problems: _____   Total Correct: _____   Score: _____

Name _____

Study the box below. Determine the correct fraction for each problem. Then, write the answer on the line provided.

Rule:	**Example:**
To determine a fraction for parts of a group, first find the total number of items in the group.	Stacy has 20 students in her class. There are 11 girls and 9 boys. What fraction of the class is boys?
This total will always be the denominator, the number that is on the bottom.	**Answer:** $\frac{9}{20}$ There are 20 students, and 9 out of 20 are boys.

1. Stuart has a vegetable garden growing in his yard. From it he picked the following vegetables: 3 tomatoes, 4 cucumbers, 5 zucchini, 3 squash, 2 peppers, and 3 carrots. Write the fraction of each vegetable he picked.

   A. tomatoes _____   D. squash _____

   B. cucumbers _____   E. peppers _____

   C. zucchini _____   F. carrots _____

2. Juan opened his bag of multi-colored candy, dumped it on the table, and counted how many pieces of each color he had. He counted 12 blue pieces, 14 red, 8 orange, 6 green, 9 yellow, and 5 brown. Write the fraction of each color he counted.

   A. blue _____   D. green _____

   B. red _____   E. yellow _____

   C. orange _____   F. brown _____

3. Mrs. King has just finished sorting the books in her class library. She has 35 fiction and 28 nonfiction books. Write the fraction of each type of book.

   A. fiction _____   B. nonfiction _____

Total Problems:	Total Correct:	Score:

49

Name _____

Study the box below. Then, compare the fractions using <, >, or =. In the square provided, place the symbol that would make each number sentence true.

Rules:

When comparing two fractions with the same denominator, compare their numerators, the numbers that are on top.

When comparing fractions that have different denominators, it may help to draw a diagram to compare them.

Examples:

6 is greater than 4

$\frac{6}{10}$ > $\frac{4}{10}$

$\frac{1}{3}$ < $\frac{3}{6}$

1. $\frac{2}{3}$ ☐ $\frac{1}{3}$

2. $\frac{5}{9}$ ☐ $\frac{6}{9}$

3. $\frac{10}{12}$ ☐ $\frac{10}{12}$

4. $\frac{1}{4}$ ☐ $\frac{2}{4}$

5. $\frac{2}{5}$ ☐ $\frac{4}{5}$

6. $\frac{12}{13}$ ☐ $\frac{11}{13}$

7. $\frac{2}{6}$ ☐ $\frac{3}{6}$

8. $\frac{5}{7}$ ☐ $\frac{6}{7}$

9. $\frac{6}{8}$ ☐ $\frac{7}{8}$

10. $\frac{1}{3}$ ☐ $\frac{1}{6}$

11. $\frac{1}{12}$ ☐ $\frac{1}{3}$

12. $\frac{1}{5}$ ☐ $\frac{7}{10}$

13. $\frac{1}{4}$ ☐ $\frac{1}{8}$

14. $\frac{1}{5}$ ☐ $\frac{1}{5}$

15. $\frac{1}{6}$ ☐ $\frac{1}{8}$

Total Problems: _____ Total Correct: _____ Score: _____

Name _____

Study the box below. Then, solve each problem. Write the answer in the space provided.

Rules:	Examples:
To find $\dfrac{1}{2}$ of a number, divide by 2.	$\dfrac{1}{2}$ of 12 is **6**
To find $\dfrac{1}{3}$ of a number, divide by 3.	$\dfrac{1}{3}$ of 12 is **4**
To find $\dfrac{1}{4}$ of a number, divide by 4.	$\dfrac{1}{4}$ of 12 is **3**

1. $\dfrac{1}{2}$ of 10 =

2. $\dfrac{1}{3}$ of 15 =

3. $\dfrac{1}{2}$ of 30 =

4. $\dfrac{1}{4}$ of 8 =

5. $\dfrac{1}{3}$ of 9 =

6. $\dfrac{1}{5}$ of 25 =

7. $\dfrac{1}{2}$ of 18 =

8. $\dfrac{1}{6}$ of 24 =

9. $\dfrac{1}{4}$ of 16 =

10. $\dfrac{1}{7}$ of 14 =

11. $\dfrac{1}{5}$ of 20 =

12. $\dfrac{1}{8}$ of 48 =

Total Problems: _____ **Total Correct:** _____ **Score:** _____

Name _____

Study the box below. Then, solve each problem. Write the answer in the space provided. Pay careful attention to the sign.

Rule:	Examples:
When adding or subtracting fractions with the same denominator:	$\dfrac{3}{8} + \dfrac{2}{8} = \dfrac{5}{8}$
First, add or subtract their numerators.	
Then, write that number over the same denominator.	$\dfrac{9}{10} - \dfrac{3}{10} = \dfrac{6}{10}$

1. $\dfrac{4}{7} - \dfrac{2}{7} =$

2. $\dfrac{3}{11} + \dfrac{5}{11} =$

3. $\dfrac{9}{14} - \dfrac{8}{14} =$

4. $\dfrac{3}{20} + \dfrac{4}{20} =$

5. $\dfrac{4}{5} - \dfrac{3}{5} =$

6. $\dfrac{1}{3} + \dfrac{1}{3} =$

7. $\dfrac{10}{25} - \dfrac{3}{25} =$

8. $\dfrac{1}{4} + \dfrac{2}{4} =$

9. $\dfrac{7}{12} - \dfrac{2}{12} =$

10. $\dfrac{5}{16} + \dfrac{4}{16} =$

11. $\dfrac{7}{8} - \dfrac{5}{8} =$

12. $\dfrac{1}{5} - \dfrac{1}{5} =$

13. $\dfrac{5}{15} - \dfrac{1}{15} =$

14. $\dfrac{1}{10} + \dfrac{3}{10} =$

15. $\dfrac{9}{15} - \dfrac{4}{15} =$

Total Problems: _____ Total Correct: _____ Score: _____

Solve the word problems. Show your work and write the answers in the space provided.

1. Marissa cut her apple pie into eighths, and she served 5 pieces to her guests for dessert. Did she serve more or less than half the pie?

2. Jake ordered a pizza and asked for it to be cut into sixths. Maurice also ordered a pizza, but he asked for it to be cut into eighths. Who had larger pieces?

3. Each child received $\frac{1}{3}$ of the 15 marbles needed to play a game. How many did each child receive?

4. Cara had 10 pieces of paper. She used 2 in math class and 3 in English. What fraction of paper did she use?

5. There are 24 students in Martel's class. Half of them are boys. How many boys are in his class?

6. David has 30 shirts in his closet. One-third of them have long sleeves. How many long-sleeved shirts does he have?

7. Reese cut the pan of brownies into eighths. He ate $\frac{3}{8}$ of the pan, and his friend ate $\frac{2}{8}$. What fraction of the brownies did they eat in all? What fraction was left over?

8. Brent's Automotive Store sold $\frac{2}{5}$ of its tires on Monday and $\frac{1}{5}$ of its tires on Tuesday. What fraction of tires was sold?

Total Problems: _____ **Total Correct:** _____ **Score:** _____

Name _____

Study the box below. Then, follow the directions.

Rule:	Example:
The decimal point separates the ones digit from the tenths digit.	**21.45 =**

2	1	.4	5
tens	ones	tenths	hundredths

Underline the digit in the tenths place.

1. 38.15   **3.** 11.18   **5.** 65.56   **7.** 50.63

2. 10.93   **4.** 9.95   **6.** 19.81   **8.** 19.58

Underline the digit in the hundredths place.

9. 19.62   **11.** 6.78   **13.** 73.17   **15.** 35.18

10. 25.84   **12.** 22.15   **14.** 99.99   **16.** 18.33

Write the place value of the 6 in each number.

17. 16.85   **20.** 18.65   **23.** 93.06   **26.** 45.6

_____

18. 11.63   **21.** 68.19   **24.** 15.64   **27.** 63.05

_____

19. 9.56   **22.** 26.51   **25.** 6.19   **28.** 46.51

_____

Total Problems:	Total Correct:	Score:

Study the example below. Read each problem. Then, write the number in decimal form on the line provided.

> **Example:**
>
> six and five-tenths is written **6.5**

1. two-tenths _____
2. five-tenths _____
3. nine-hundredths _____
4. six-hundredths _____
5. three and one-tenth _____
6. seven-tenths _____

7. one and nine-hundredths _____
8. four and six-tenths _____
9. fifteen and eight-hundredths _____
10. ninety-three-hundredths _____
11. seventeen-hundredths _____
12. three and eleven-hundredths _____

Study the examples below. Read each problem. Then, write the decimal in word form on the line provided.

> **Examples:**
>
> 1.8 = **one and eight-tenths**   0.56 = **fifty-six-hundredths**

13. 0.6 _____
14. 0.06 _____
15. 2.8 _____
16. 0.13 _____
17. 0.35 _____
18. 4.04 _____
19. 0.9 _____

20. 0.02 _____
21. 4.17 _____
22. 0.57 _____
23. 5.57 _____
24. 0.5 _____
25. 0.1 _____
26. 2.12 _____

Total Problems: _____   **Total Correct:** _____   **Score:** _____

Study the box below. Compare the decimals using < , > , or =. Place the correct symbol in each square.

Rule:	Example:
To compare two or more decimals:	1.3 ☐ 1.4
Line up the decimal points.	$\left.\begin{array}{l}1.3\\1.4\end{array}\right\}$ 3 is less than 4, so
Compare digits from left to right in their corresponding place value positions.	1.3 **<** 1.4

1.   0.6 ☐ 0.7

2.   2.3 ☐ 2.3

3.   0.72 ☐ 0.67

4.   4.3 ☐ 4.5

5.   0.6 ☐ 0.60

6.   0.45 ☐ 0.39

7.   0.52 ☐ 0.25

8.   7.6 ☐ 7.60

Order the decimals from least to greatest.

9.   0.5   0.4   0.2

_____

10.   3.7   3.5   3.8

_____

11.   30.7   28.4   29.1

_____

12.   0.62   0.63   0.4

_____

13.   0.86   0.6   1.3

_____

14.   9.9   9   9.99

_____

Total Problems: _____   Total Correct: _____   Score: _____

Study the box below. Then, solve the problems and write the answers in the space provided.

Rule:	Example:
1. Line up the decimal points.	$3.76 + 1.59 =$
2. Start from the far right.	
3. Regroup as needed.	
4. Bring the decimal point down to the answer.	

$$3.76 + 1.59$$

$$\begin{array}{r} \overset{1\ 1}{3.76} \\ + 1.59 \\ \hline 5\ 35 \end{array} \qquad \begin{array}{r} \overset{1\ 1}{3.76} \\ + 1.59 \\ \hline \mathbf{5.35} \end{array}$$

1.
$$\begin{array}{r} 6.5 \\ + 7.3 \\ \hline \end{array}$$

6.
$$\begin{array}{r} 5.9 \\ - 2.5 \\ \hline \end{array}$$

11.
$$\begin{array}{r} 2.41 \\ + 7.49 \\ \hline \end{array}$$

16.
$$\begin{array}{r} 10.5 \\ - 7.7 \\ \hline \end{array}$$

2.
$$\begin{array}{r} 2.7 \\ + 4.1 \\ \hline \end{array}$$

7.
$$\begin{array}{r} 12.5 \\ + 9.4 \\ \hline \end{array}$$

12.
$$\begin{array}{r} 5.7 \\ + 8.5 \\ \hline \end{array}$$

17.
$$\begin{array}{r} 4.13 \\ - 2.95 \\ \hline \end{array}$$

3.
$$\begin{array}{r} 6.5 \\ - 1.2 \\ \hline \end{array}$$

8.
$$\begin{array}{r} 0.42 \\ + 0.36 \\ \hline \end{array}$$

13.
$$\begin{array}{r} 3.8 \\ + 4.9 \\ \hline \end{array}$$

18.
$$\begin{array}{r} 0.28 \\ + .87 \\ \hline \end{array}$$

4.
$$\begin{array}{r} 3.8 \\ - 2.7 \\ \hline \end{array}$$

9.
$$\begin{array}{r} 9.8 \\ - 7.3 \\ \hline \end{array}$$

14.
$$\begin{array}{r} 0.59 \\ - 0.18 \\ \hline \end{array}$$

19.
$$\begin{array}{r} 4.79 \\ + 5.75 \\ \hline \end{array}$$

5.
$$\begin{array}{r} 0.2 \\ + 0.5 \\ \hline \end{array}$$

10.
$$\begin{array}{r} 6.7 \\ - 4.7 \\ \hline \end{array}$$

15.
$$\begin{array}{r} 3.86 \\ + 1.39 \\ \hline \end{array}$$

20.
$$\begin{array}{r} 1.2 \\ - 0.5 \\ \hline \end{array}$$

Solve the word problems. Show your work and write the answers in the space provided.

1. Camilla was taking a math test. Her teacher asked her to write the decimal two and three tenths. She wrote **2.03**. Did she write the decimal correctly? If not, correct it.

5. Mrs. Watson bought each of her two children a bag of popcorn at the movies for $0.79 per bag. How much money did she spend in all for the popcorn?

2. Write thirteen and sixty-three-hundredths. Circle the digit in the tenths place.

6. Write twenty and seventy-hundredths. Circle the digit in the tenths place.

3. Complete the next 3 decimals in each sequence.

   A.   .15, .25, .35, .45, _____ , _____ , _____

   B.   3.8, 3.7, 3.6, 3.5, _____ , _____ , _____

7. Using the greater than (>) and less than (<) symbols, write two number sentences with the following numbers.

   3.4, 3.5

4. Place the following numbers in order from least to greatest.

   2.5, 5.2, 4.2, 4.12, 5.25

8. Chuck's weekly allowance is $5.00. After buying a package of beef jerky for $1.67, how much money does he have left?

Total Problems: _____   Total Correct: _____   Score: _____

Name _____

Read each clock. Using numerals, write the time on the line provided. Remember to correctly label each clock with A.M. or P.M.

1.   Wake Up

_____

2.   School Starts

8:15

_____

3.   Bedtime

8:45

_____

4.   Lunch

_____

5.   Recess

_____

6.   Baseball Game

_____

7.   Reading Group

2:15

_____

8.   Swim Lesson

_____

9.   Dinner

7:00

_____

Name _____

Elapsed Time

Find each time. All times are A.M. Write the answer on the line provided.

1. 30 minutes after

5:00

3. 15 minutes after

4:3̶45

5. 30 minutes before

8:0̶

2. 15 minutes after

11:30

4. 30 minutes after

2:45

6. 1 hour before

5:00

7. 30 minutes after 7:05 P.M. _____

11. 1 hour after 1:30 P.M. _____

8. 20 minutes after 9:10 A.M. _____

12. 45 minutes before 4:15 P.M. _____

9. 1 hour and 30 minutes
before 3:15 P.M. _____

13. 1 hour and 15 minutes
after 9:10 A.M. _____

10. 45 minutes after 2:15 P.M. _____

14. 30 minutes after 3:45 P.M. _____

60

| Total Problems: | Total Correct: | Score: |

Name _____

Mrs. Simms has 2 children, Jay and Joy. The calendar shows Jay's baseball games and Joy's soccer games in April. Use the calendar to answer the questions.

April

Sunday	Monday	Tuesday	Wednesday	Thursday	Friday	Saturday
		1 Jay's Game	2	3 Joy's Game	4	5 Jay's & Joy's Games
6	7 Jay's Game	8 Joy's Game	9	10 Joy's Game	11	12 Joy's Game
13 Jay's Game	14	15 Jay's Game	16	17 Joy's Game	18	19 Jay's & Joy's Games
20	21	22 Jay's Game	23	24 Joy's Game	25 Joy's Game	26 Jay's Game
27	28	29 Jay's Game	30			

1. Who plays the first game of the month?

   _____

2. What day of the week is the first game?

   _____

3. Who has more games, Jay or Joy?

   _____

4. Who has a game on the second Tuesday of the month?

   _____

5. On April 24, Joy has a game. What day of the week is that?

   _____

6. How many games does Joy play on Tuesdays and Saturdays?

   _____

7. On which dates do both Jay and Joy have games?

   _____

8. A week begins on Sunday and ends on Saturday. In which week are the most games played?

   _____

9. Are there any days of the week in which no games are played?

   _____

Total Problems:	Total Correct:	Score:

Solve the word problems. Show your work and write the answers in the space provided.

1. Maya's class ate lunch at 12:00 P.M. If they had 30 minutes to eat, what time did they finish?

4. Ayesha's baby brother was born at 12:45 P.M. on 7/11/90. Was he born before or after noon? What month and year was he born?

2. Is the following statement true or false? If false, rewrite it correctly. When it is 10:30, the hour hand is between the 9 and 10.

5. Daria's birthday party lasted 2 hours and 30 minutes. The party ended at 4:00 P.M. What time did it begin?

3. Malcolm went to play at a friend's house. He left at 4:00 P.M. and was told to be home in $1\frac{1}{2}$ hours. What time should he arrive home?

6. David took his dogs on a walk from 5:30 to 6:15. Was that less than 1 hour or more than 1 hour?

Total Problems: _____   Total Correct: _____   Score: _____

Add or subtract each problem. Remember to include a decimal point (.) and a dollar sign ($) or a cent sign (¢) in each answer. Write the answer in the space provided.

1. $4.55 + $0.12	7. $7.95 + $5.05	13. $29.99 + $13.95	19. $619.00 + $225.53
2. $6.70 – $0.50	8. 89¢ – 64¢	14. $57.00 + $19.75	20. $475.00 – $199.99
3. 65¢ + 25¢	9. $6.45 + $3.60	15. $29.53 + $18.19	21. $672.00 – $480.65
4. $10.30 – $10.10	10. $5.10 – $4.90	16. $151.09 – $16.10	22. $781.50 – $781.39
5. $5.05 + $6.13	11. $63.89 + $12.55	17. $905.00 – $675.60	23. $499.75 + $ 399.75
6. $8.88 – $7.77	12. $19.85 – $10.70	18. $590.50 + $195.50	24. $650.03 + $185.07

Total Problems: _____   Total Correct: _____   Score: _____

Using only pennies, nickels, dimes, and quarters, what is the fewest number of coins that will make each amount below? Write the answer on the line provided.

1. $0.30 _____ coins   4. $0.70 _____ coins   7. $0.85 _____ coins

2. $0.10 _____ coins   5. $0.62 _____ coins   8. $0.90 _____ coins

3. $0.45 _____ coins   6. $0.38 _____ coins   9. $0.98 _____ coins

Solve the word problems. Show your work and write the answers in the space provided.

10. Rebekah rented a movie that cost $3.79. She gave the clerk $4.00. What was her change?

13. Mark bought a pack of gum for $0.35 and a candy bar for $0.45. He gave the clerk $1.00. What was his change?

11. Rachel bought a magazine for $1.98. She gave the clerk $2.00. What was her change?

14. Leigh purchased a doll for $19.59. She gave the clerk $20.00. What was her change?

12. Rob bought an action figure for his collection. He gave the clerk a $20 bill for the $19.75 figure. What was his change?

15. Seth bought a soda from the vending machine. It was $0.55. He put in 3 quarters. What was his change?

Total Problems: _____ Total Correct: _____ Score: _____

Read the problems below. Then, circle the letter beside the correct amount of change.

1. Erin gave the clerk $10.00 for a hair clip that cost $7.95.

   A. $1.05   B. $2.05   C. $3.05

5. Tameka gave the clerk $25.00 for a jumper that cost $22.59.

   A. $2.41   B. $2.51   C. $2.61

2. Lance gave the clerk $5.00 for an item that cost $3.50.

   A. $1.50   B. $2.50   C. $3.50

6. Ada gave the cashier $30.00 for a board game that cost $22.71.

   A. $6.29   B. $7.19   C. $7.29

3. Lamont gave the clerk $5.00 for groceries that cost $3.99.

   A. $0.01   B. $1.01   C. $2.01

7. Lily gave the cashier $50.00 for a phone that cost $29.50.

   A. $11.50   B. $20.50   C. $21.50

4. Carrie gave the clerk $20.00 for a shirt that cost $16.78.

   A. $3.12   B. $3.22   C. $4.22

8. George gave the cashier $100.00 for a painting that cost $71.85.

   A. $28.15   B. $28.05   C. $38.15

Total Problems: **Total Correct:**   **Score:**

Solve the word problems. Show your work and write the answers in the space provided.

1. Andrew has 3 dimes, 3 nickels, and 7 pennies. Does he have enough money to buy a soda for 50¢?

Yes

5. Sarah paid $29.95 for a video game. Her friend Melissa bought the same game for $27.99. How much more did Sarah pay for the game?

$2.04 ¢

2. Elli had 3 quarters, 1 dime, 2 nickels, and 6 pennies. Did she have more or less than 1 dollar?

more than
I dollar

6. Tony gave the clerk $1.00 for a cookie that cost 89¢. How much change did Tony receive?

11¢

3. Liz bought popcorn for $1.89, candy for $1.79, and a soda for 99¢. How much money did she spend?

```
  2 2
  1.89    $4.67
  1.79
   .99
  4.67
```

7. Shayla purchased a video game for $33.54. She gave the clerk $35.04. How much change did she receive?

```
  $35.04.
  33.54.
  345 0
```

4. Karlton has admired a 10-speed bicycle for a few months. So far he has saved $45.75. The bike costs $79. How much more money does he need to purchase the bike?

$8.25¢

8. Lucia had 3 dollars, 3 quarters, 8 dimes, 5 nickels, and 6 pennies. Did she have more or less than 5 dollars?

4.80
.80

less

Total Problems: 8   Total Correct: 5   Score: C-

Name _____

Using a centimeter ruler, measure each line segment to the nearest centimeter. Write the answer in the space to the right of the segment.

1. _____

2. _____

3. _____

4. _____

5. ____

6. _____

Study the box below. Then, answer "yes" or "no" to each question, on the line provided.

Rules:	Example:
1 centimeter (cm) = 10 millimeters (mm) 1 decimeter (dm) = 10 centimeters 1 meter (m) = 100 centimeters 1 km (km) = 1,000 meters	Is 1 m longer than 120 cm? 1 m = 100 cm, so 1 meter is not longer than 120 cm. Answer: **No**

7. Is 15 cm longer than 1 dm? _____

8. Is 900 m longer than 1 km? _____

9. Is 1 m longer than 1 dm? _____

10. Is 5 mm longer than 1 cm? _____

11. Is 2 cm longer than 10 mm? _____

12. Is 5 dm longer than 1 m? _____

13. Is 1 m longer than 90 cm? _____

14. Is 20 cm longer than 1 m? _____

15. Is 2 km longer than 1,500 m? _____

16. Is 15 dm longer than 1 m? _____

Total Problems: _____   Total Correct: _____   Score: _____

Name _____

Using an inch ruler, measure each segment to the nearest inch. Write the answer in the space to the right of the segment.

1. _____

2. _____

3. _____

4. _____

5. _____

6. _____

Study the box below. Then, answer "yes" or "no" to each question on the line provided.

Rules:	Example:
12 inches = 1 foot	Are there 24 inches in 2 feet?
3 feet or 36 inches = 1 yard	If there are 12 inches in 1 foot, then there are
5,280 feet = 1 mile	24 inches in 2 feet (12 x 2).
	Answer: **Yes**

7. Are there 3 yards in 1 foot? _____

8. Are there 3 feet in 1 yard? _____

9. Are there 38 inches in 1 yard? _____

10. Is 1 mile longer than 4,900 feet? _____

11. Is 36 inches equal to 3 feet? _____

12. Is 3 yards longer than 9 feet? _____

13. Are there 6 feet in 2 yards? _____

14. Are there 2 miles in 1,000 feet? _____

15. Are there 12 inches in 1 foot? _____

16. Is 2 feet longer than 1 yard? _____

68

Total Problems:	Total Correct:	Score:

Name _____

Study the rules below. Then, determine which measurement seems reasonable and circle the answer.

Rules:	
milliliter (ml) used to measure very small amounts of liquid	**liter (l)** 1 liter = 1,000 milliliters used to measure average amounts of liquid

1.   eyedropper

    2 ml   2 l

2.   bucket

    10 ml   10 l

3.   coffee cup

    40 ml   4 l

4.   bathtub

    80 ml   80 l

5.   teaspoon

    3 ml   3 l

6.   teakettle

    2 ml   2 l

Study the rules below. Then, determine whether each object should be measured in grams or kilograms. Write the answer on the line provided.

Rules:	
gram (g) used to measure smaller objects	**kilogram (kg)** 1kg = 1,000 g used to measure larger objects

7.   paper clip _____

8.   dog _____

9.   chair _____

10. empty bucket _____

11. bucket of water _____

12. pencil _____

13. watermelon _____

14. letter _____

Total Problems: _____   Total Correct: _____   Score: _____

Study the box below. Then, complete each sentence using "more than," "less than," or "equal to." Write the answer on the line provided.

Rules:	Example:
2 cups = 1 pint	If 2 cups = 1 pint,
2 pints = 1 quart	then,
4 quarts = 1 gallon	1 cup is __**less than**__ 1 pint.

1. 2 pints are _____ 1 quart.

2. 3 quarts are _____ 1 gallon.

3. 1 gallon is _____ 1 pint.

4. 2 pints are _____ 4 cups.

5. 1 pint is _____ 1 quart.

6. 3 cups are _____ 1 quart.

7. 6 pints are _____ 3 quarts.

8. 8 quarts are _____ 2 gallons.

Study the rules below. Then, determine whether each object should be measured in pounds or ounces. Write the answer on the line provided.

Rules:	
ounce (oz) used to measure smaller objects	**pound (lb)** used to measure larger objects

9. piece of cheese _____

10. set of encyclopedias _____

11. bookcase _____

12. pencil _____

13. plate _____

14. refrigerator _____

Total Problems:	Total Correct:	Score:

Solve the word problems. Show your work and write the answers in the space provided.

1. Miranda's teddy bear has a width of 10 inches and a length of 20 inches. Which measurement is longer than 1 foot?

5. You have two buckets. One bucket holds 6 liters of water, and the other holds 4 liters. How can you use these buckets to measure 2 liters of water?

2. Would you use inches, feet, or miles to measure the length of a school bus?

6. Lawrence wants 2 lbs of roast beef. The scale reads 14 oz. Does he have enough? If not, how much more does he need? (Hint: 1 lb = 16 oz)

3. If there are 1,000 meters in 1 kilometer, how many meters are in 2 kilometers? Explain how you reached your answer.

7. A can of soda has 385 ml of liquid. How many cans would you need to have 1 liter of soda? (Hint: 1,000 ml = 1 l)

4. Isabella needs 3 gallons of water to make lemonade. If all she has is a 1-quart container to measure the water, how many times will she have to fill the container to get 3 gallons of water? (Hint: 1 gal = 4 qt)

8. The mass of a dollar bill is about 1 g. Would 2,000 dollar bills weigh more or less than 1 kilogram? (Hint: 1 kg = 1,000 g)

Total Problems: _____   Total Correct: _____   Score: _____

Study the box below. Then, determine whether each figure has a line of symmetry. If it does, draw it. If it doesn't, write "none" on the line below it.

Rule:

A **line of symmetry** cuts a figure in half so that you see exactly the same image on each side of the line.

Example:

1.

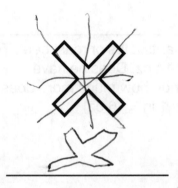
_____

4.

none
_____

7.

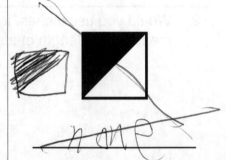

none
_____

2.

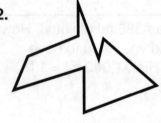

none
_____

5.

none
_____

8.

_____

3.

_____

6.

_____

9.

_____

| Total Problems: | Total Correct: | Score: |

Study the box below. Then, determine whether each pair of figures is congruent. Write "yes" or "no" in the space provided.

Rule:	**Examples:**
Figures are **congruent** when they have the same size and shape.	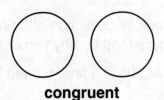 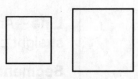
	congruent not congruent

1.
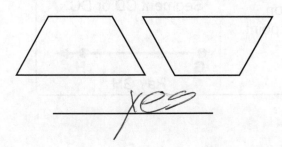

yes

5.
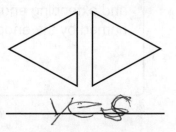

yes

2.

no

6.
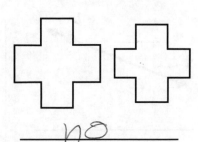

no

3.

yes

7.
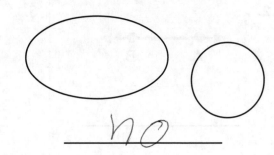

no

4.
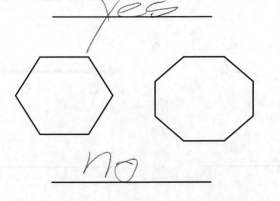

no

8.
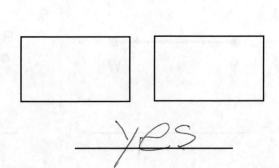

yes

Total Problems: 8   **Total Correct:** 8   **Score:** 8

Name _____

Study the box below. Then, label each figure as a line, segment, or ray. Write the answer on the line provided. Remember to include the points in each answer.

Rules:

Line – An endless collection of points along a straight path, named by any two of its points.

Segment – A part of a line, named by its two endpoints.

Ray – A part of a line having one endpoint and extending endlessly in one direction, named by the endpoint and one other point.

Examples:

Line EF or FE

Segment CD or DC

Ray GH

1.

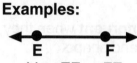

_____

2.

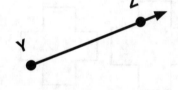

_____

3.

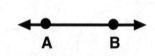

_____

4.

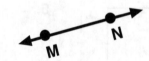

_____

5.

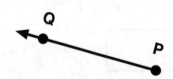

_____

6.

_____

7.

_____

8.

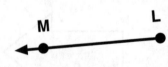

_____

9.

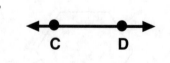

_____

Total Problems: _____ Total Correct: _____ Score: _____

Study the box below. Then, find the area and perimeter of each figure. Write the answer on the line provided.

Rules:

Area (A) is the number of square units inside a figure. To find the area of rectangles and squares, multiply the length times the width.

Perimeter (P) is the number of units around a figure. To find the perimeter of rectangles and squares, add the number of squares on each side.

Examples:

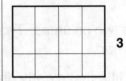

A = 4 x 3 = **12 square units**
P = 4 + 3 + 4 + 3 = **14 units**

1.

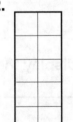

Area: _____

Perimeter: _____

5.

Area: _____

Perimeter: _____

2.

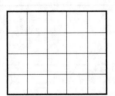

Area: _____

Perimeter: _____

6.

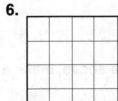

Area: _____

Perimeter: _____

3.

Area: _____

Perimeter: _____

7.

Area: _____

Perimeter: _____

4.

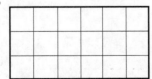

Area: _____

Perimeter: _____

8.

Area: _____

Perimeter: _____

Using the data in the box below, make a table in the space provided.

Tips:	Data:
You should have two columns: *Type of Pet* and *Number Owned*. Give the table a title that clearly describes the information shown in the table.	This is a list of pets owned by the students in Rachel's class: dog, dog, dog, cat, bird, cat, cat, bird, fish, bird, guinea pig, dog, dog, dog, cat, bird.

Using the table you've made above, make a bar graph in the space provided to display the information.

Tips:
1. Label the left side and bottom.
2. Number the graph so that all the data can be graphed.
3. Draw the bars.
4. Give the graph a title which describes the information shown.

Total Problems:	Total Correct:	Score:

Study the rule below. Decide whether the following outcomes are certain (will definitely happen), possible (might happen), or impossible (will not happen). Then, write the answer on the line provided.

> **Rule:**
> An outcome is the result of an event.

1. It will rain tomorrow.   _____

2. You will grow to 50 feet tall.   _____

3. The Falcons will win the Super Bowl next season.   _____

4. In a drawer full of black socks, you will pick out a white pair.   _____

5. Tomorrow will be 24 hours long.   _____

6. Humans will travel to Mars.   _____

7. New Year's Eve will fall on December 31st.   _____

8. In a box of raisins, you will pick out a peanut.   _____

9. Ice will make your drink cold.   _____

10. It will snow in Denver, Colorado, on December 21st.   _____

11. Every kernel will pop in a bag of popcorn.   _____

12. It will rain every Monday in Provo, Utah, for a full year.   _____

13. The sun will set in the west.   _____

14. Water will boil at 50 degrees Fahrenheit.   _____

Solve the word problems in the space provided.

1. The following data indicates student absences for one day at a typical school:
    6th grade – 13 absent; 7th grade – 9 absent; 8th grade – 9 absent. Use this information to make a table.

2. Using the data from problem 1, make a bar graph showing the absences in each grade.

3. Suppose you want to offer cookies to friends who have come to your house after school. Which question would be more helpful to ask your guests before you go to the kitchen to get the cookies? Why?

    A. Which cookie do you like best?

    B. Which cookie would you prefer—chocolate, oatmeal raisin, or sugar?

4. In the weather forecaster's report, she says, "There is a slight chance of rain tomorrow." What does this mean?

Total Problems: _____   Total Correct: _____   Score: _____

Place Value

Name _____

Study the example below. Write the value of each underlined digit on the line provided.

Example:

Millions			Thousands			Ones		
Hundred Millions	Ten Millions	Millions	Hundred Thousands	Ten Thousands	Thousands	Hundreds	Tens	Ones
5	0	3,	6	7	3,	9	8	2

The underlined digit **9** is in the hundreds place; therefore, it has a value of **900**.

1. 6̲8
   60

2. 2̲03
   3

3. 3̲56
   300

4. 278̲
   8

5. 4̲56
   50

6. 2,3̲48
   300

7. 4̲,438
   4,000

8. 37̲,894
   30,000

9. 62,8̲05
   800

10. 9̲42,018
    900,000

11. 164,3̲88
    4,000

12. 23̲6,195
    30,000

13. 687,3̲20
    300

14. 5̲,941,603
    5,000,000

15. 7,4̲38,821
    400,000

Total Problems: ___ Total Correct: ___ Score: ___   **9**

Reading and Writing Numbers

Name _____

Study the box below. Then, write each number in standard numerical form on the line provided.

Rule:	Examples:
A number is usually written using digits in the appropriate place value spots. This is called standard form.	five thousand, two hundred fifty-one = **5,251** twenty-two thousand, thirty-three = **22,033**

1. six hundred thirty-four =
   634

2. eight thousand, two hundred fifty-one =
   8,251

3. nine thousand, three hundred twenty-two =
   9,322

4. twenty-seven thousand, eight hundred =
   27,800

5. seventy thousand, one hundred two =
   70,102

6. eighty-three thousand, three hundred eleven =
   83,311

7. seven hundred eighty-two thousand, sixteen =
   782,016

8. four hundred thousand =
   400,000

9. two hundred fourteen thousand, five hundred three =
   214,503

10. nine hundred eight thousand, five hundred two =
    908,502

11. sixty one thousand, five =
    61,005

12. one hundred forty thousand, fifteen =
    140,015

13. eighty-one thousand, three hundred twelve =
    81,312

14. seven thousand, ninety =
    7,090

10   Total Problems: ___ Total Correct: ___ Score: ___

Expanded Notation

Name _____

Study the box below. For each problem, circle the letter beside the correct answer.

Rule:	Examples:
Expanded notation is writing a number to show the value of each digit in the number.	583 = **500 + 80 + 3** Six hundred fifty-two = **600 + 50 + 2**

1. Eight hundred seventy-five =
   A. 8,000 + 75
   B. 800 + 75
   C. 80,000 + 700 + 50
   D. 800,000 + 75

2. Six thousand, forty-eight =
   A. 6,000 + 400 + 80
   B. 10,000 + 6,000 + 400 + 80
   C. 6,000 + 40 + 8
   D. 60,000 + 40 + 8

3. Eighteen thousand, five hundred seven =
   A. 10,000 + 8,000 + 500 + 7
   B. 1,000 + 800 + 20 + 7
   C. 10,000 + 8,000 + 500 + 70
   D. 10,000 + 50 + 7

4. 700 + 30 + 6 =
   A. 17,360
   B. 7,063
   C. 736
   D. 7,036

5. 9,000 + 400 + 20 + 8 =
   A. 928
   B. 9,128
   C. 94,208
   D. 9,428

6. 50,000 + 9,000 + 600 + 40 + 1 =
   A. 5,964
   B. 59,641
   C. 596,401
   D. 802,135

Total Problems: ___ Total Correct: ___ Score: ___   **11**

Comparing and Ordering Numbers

Name _____

Study the examples below. To compare each pair of numbers, use less than (<), greater than (>), or equal to (=). Place the symbol in the square provided.

Examples: 375 **<** 475   7,000 **=** 7,000   3,482 **>** 2,843

1. 620 **<** 6,200
2. 493 **>** 439
3. 6,432 **<** 16,408
4. 9,286 **<** 13,489
5. 724 **=** 724
6. 3,080 **<** 3,800
7. 45,015 **<** 45,016
8. 397,124 **>** 387,425
9. 488,188 **>** 488,018

Study the example below. On the line provided, order each set of numbers from least to greatest.

Example:
The series 235, 462, 183 would be properly ordered as **183, 235, 462**.

10. 43, 28, 17
    17, 28, 42

11. 623, 185, 94
    94, 185, 623

12. 613, 419, 582
    419, 582, 613

13. 101, 110, 210, 109
    101, 109, 110, 210

14. 751, 739, 839, 749
    739, 749, 751, 839

15. 450, 449, 339, 180
    180, 339, 449, 450

16. 4,810; 6,412; 3,789; 6,413
    3,789; 4,810; 6,412; 6,413

17. 5,725; 7,415; 4,535; 6,845
    4,535; 5,725; 6,845; 7,415

12   Total Problems: ___ Total Correct: ___ Score: ___

Rounding to the Nearest 10

Name _____

Study the box below. Round each number to the nearest 10. Then, write the answer on the line provided.

Rule:	Examples:
Round numbers to the nearest 10 by checking the digit in the ones place value spot.	43 rounds to **40**
If that digit is 5 or greater, round up to the next 10. If it is 4 or lower, keep the same 10 and change the ones digit to a 0.	68 rounds to **70**
	439 rounds to **440**

1. 46 rounds to __50__
2. 338 rounds to __340__
3. 84 rounds to __80__
4. 32 rounds to __30__
5. 235 rounds to __240__
6. 168 rounds to __170__
7. 349 rounds to __350__
8. 1,475 rounds to __1,480__
9. 3,188 rounds to __3,190__
10. 2,081 rounds to __2,080__
11. 4,111 rounds to __4,110__
12. 6,285 rounds to __6,290__
13. 8,522 rounds to __8,520__
14. 5,477 rounds to __5,480__
15. 7,284 rounds to __7,280__
16. 9,666 rounds to __9,6700__

Total Problems: ___ Total Correct: ___ Score: ___ **13**

© Carson-Dellosa CD-2210

Rounding to the Nearest 100

Name _____

Study the box below. Round each number to the nearest 100. Then, write the answer on the line provided.

Rule:	Examples:
Round numbers to the nearest 100 by checking the digit in the tens place value spot.	132 rounds to **100**
If that digit is 5 or greater, round up to the next 100. If it is 4 or lower, keep the same 100. Remember to change the ones and tens digits to 0.	364 rounds to **400**
	5,682 rounds to **5,700**

1. 284 rounds to __300__
2. 443 rounds to __400__
3. 538 rounds to __500__
4. 651 rounds to __700__
5. 894 rounds to __900__
6. 777 rounds to __800__
7. 326 rounds to __300__
8. 527 rounds to __500__
9. 152 rounds to __200__
10. 1,324 rounds to __1,300__
11. 2,861 rounds to __2,900__
12. 1,555 rounds to __1,600__
13. 4,506 rounds to __4,500__
14. 3,250 rounds to __3,300__
15. 6,875 rounds to __6,900__
16. 9,256 rounds to __9,300__

14 Total Problems: ___ Total Correct: ___ Score: ___

© Carson-Dellosa CD-2210

Problem Solving

Name _____

Solve the word problems. Show your work and write the answers in the space provided.

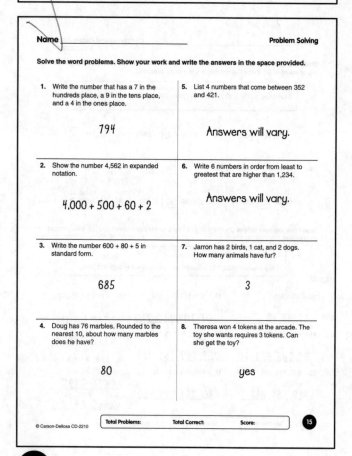

1. Write the number that has a 7 in the hundreds place, a 9 in the tens place, and a 4 in the ones place.

   794

2. Show the number 4,562 in expanded notation.

   4,000 + 500 + 60 + 2

3. Write the number 600 + 80 + 5 in standard form.

   685

4. Doug has 76 marbles. Rounded to the nearest 10, about how many marbles does he have?

   80

5. List 4 numbers that come between 352 and 421.

   Answers will vary.

6. Write 6 numbers in order from least to greatest that are higher than 1,234.

   Answers will vary.

7. Jarron has 2 birds, 1 cat, and 2 dogs. How many animals have fur?

   3

8. Theresa won 4 tokens at the arcade. The toy she wants requires 3 tokens. Can she get the toy?

   yes

© Carson-Dellosa CD-2210   Total Problems: ___ Total Correct: ___ Score: ___ **15**

Basic Addition Facts

Name _____

Add. Then, write the answer on the line provided.

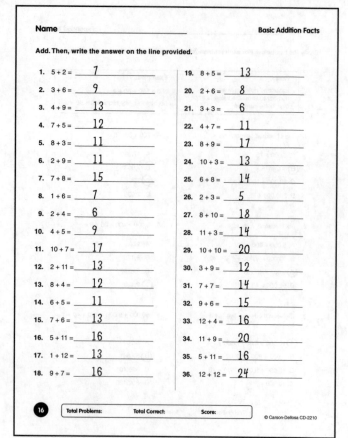

1. 5 + 2 = __7__
2. 3 + 6 = __9__
3. 4 + 9 = __13__
4. 7 + 5 = __12__
5. 8 + 3 = __11__
6. 2 + 9 = __11__
7. 7 + 8 = __15__
8. 1 + 6 = __7__
9. 2 + 4 = __6__
10. 4 + 5 = __9__
11. 10 + 7 = __17__
12. 2 + 11 = __13__
13. 8 + 4 = __12__
14. 6 + 5 = __11__
15. 7 + 6 = __13__
16. 5 + 11 = __16__
17. 1 + 12 = __13__
18. 9 + 7 = __16__
19. 8 + 5 = __13__
20. 2 + 6 = __8__
21. 3 + 3 = __6__
22. 4 + 7 = __11__
23. 8 + 9 = __17__
24. 10 + 3 = __13__
25. 6 + 8 = __14__
26. 2 + 3 = __5__
27. 8 + 10 = __18__
28. 11 + 3 = __14__
29. 10 + 10 = __20__
30. 3 + 9 = __12__
31. 7 + 7 = __14__
32. 9 + 6 = __15__
33. 12 + 4 = __16__
34. 11 + 9 = __20__
35. 5 + 11 = __16__
36. 12 + 12 = __24__

16 Total Problems: ___ Total Correct: ___ Score: ___

© Carson-Dellosa CD-2210

© Carson-Dellosa CD-2210

Worksheet 17 — Addition without Regrouping

Name _____   Addition without Regrouping

Study the box below. Solve each problem and write the answer in the space provided.

Rule:
1. Add the ones column.
2. Add the tens column.
3. Add the hundreds column.
4. Continue to add columns as needed.

Example:

132,378 + 521,421 = 9	132,378 + 521,421 = 99	132,378 + 521,421 = 799
132,378 + 521,421 = 3,799	132,378 + 521,421 = 53,799	132,378 + 521,421 = 653,799

1. $15 + 4 = 19$
2. $24 + 4 = 28$
3. $30 + 12 = 42$
4. $26 + 21 = 47$
5. $32 + 25 = 57$
6. $54 + 14 = 68$
7. $62 + 15 = 77$
8. $84 + 13 = 97$
9. $134 + 53 = 187$
10. $462 + 125 = 587$
11. $334 + 252 = 586$
12. $641 + 227 = 868$
13. $2,413 + 1,352 = 3,765$
14. $2,461 + 3,425 = 5,886$
15. $7,849 + 2,140 = 9,989$
16. $3,296 + 2,703 = 5,999$
17. $42,334 + 31,360 = 73,694$
18. $75,214 + 13,662 = 88,876$
19. $290,431 + 307,553 = 597,984$
20. $216,378 + 521,421 = 737,799$

Total Problems: Total Correct: Score: **17**

© Carson-Dellosa CD-2210

Worksheet 18 — Addition with Regrouping

Name _____   Addition with Regrouping

Study the box below. Solve each problem and write the answer in the space provided.

Rule:
1. Add the ones column, then regroup.
2. Add the tens column, then regroup.
3. Add the hundreds column, then regroup.
4. Continue to add columns and regroup as needed.

Example:

217,388 + 692,438 = 6	217,388 + 692,438 = 26	217,388 + 692,438 = 826
217,388 + 692,438 = 9,826	217,388 + 692,438 = 09,826	217,388 + 692,438 = 909,826

1. $35 + 27 = 62$
2. $28 + 14 = 42$
3. $62 + 39 = 101$
4. $72 + 49 = 121$
5. $55 + 67 = 122$
6. $85 + 56 = 141$
7. $78 + 66 = 144$
8. $97 + 45 = 142$
9. $68 + 77 = 145$
10. $239 + 164 = 403$
11. $348 + 235 = 583$
12. $565 + 217 = 782$
13. $757 + 386 = 1,143$
14. $898 + 467 = 1,365$
15. $954 + 375 = 1,329$
16. $628 + 597 = 1,225$
17. $4,188 + 176 = 4,364$
18. $5,264 + 6,478 = 11,742$
19. $2,357 + 4,991 = 7,348$
20. $37,835 + 24,638 = 62,473$

18   Total Problems: Total Correct: Score: © Carson-Dellosa CD-2210

Worksheet 19 — Adding with Two or More Addends

Name _____   Adding with Two or More Addends

Read the box below. Solve each problem. Then, write the answer in the space provided.

Tip: Keep the place values lined up properly to be sure you find the right sum.

1. $62 + 43 = 105$
2. $75 + 85 = 160$
3. $54 + 92 = 146$
4. $726 + 685 = 1,411$
5. $201 + 436 + 313 + 542 = 1,492$
6. $736 + 89 + 104 = 929$
7. $3,482 + 437 + 68 = 3,987$
8. $246 + 442 + 53 = 741$
9. $462 + 129 + 513 = 1,104$
10. $315 + 127 + 382 + 98 = 922$
11. $6,428 + 1,375 + 3,684 = 11,487$
12. $30,147 + 25,236 + 42,613 = 97,996$
13. $2,804 + 1,366 + 5,391 = 9,561$
14. $16,284 + 2,590 + 177 = 19,051$
15. $623 + 431 + 907 + 75 = 2,036$
16. $5,894 + 1,388 + 3,137 = 10,419$
17. $28,123 + 33,294 + 46,510 = 107,927$
18. $14,738 + 22,856 + 17,979 = 55,573$
19. $30,164 + 23,606 + 48,224 = 101,994$
20. $1,425 + 4,138 + 621 + 521 = 6,705$

Total Problems: Total Correct: Score: **19**

© Carson-Dellosa CD-2210

Worksheet 20 — Rounding and Estimating Sums

Name _____   Rounding and Estimating Sums

Study the examples below. Round each number to the greatest place value position. Then, write the answer on the line provided.

Examples:
25 rounds to **30**
473 rounds to **500**

1. 27 rounds to **30**
2. 83 rounds to **80**
3. 35 rounds to **40**
4. 72 rounds to **70**
5. 80 rounds to **80**
6. 96 rounds to **100**
7. 94 rounds to **90**
8. 18 rounds to **20**
9. 356 rounds to **400**
10. 782 rounds to **800**
11. 372 rounds to **400**
12. 935 rounds to **900**

Using the space to the right of each problem, round both numbers. Then, estimate each sum and write the answer in the space provided.

13. $23 + 19$ → $20 + 20 = 40$
14. $34 + 86$ → $30 + 90 = 120$
15. $45 + 23$ → $50 + 20 = 70$
16. $97 + 38$ → $100 + 40 = 140$
17. $124 + 173$ → $100 + 200 = 300$
18. $365 + 284$ → $400 + 300 = 700$
19. $419 + 477$ → $400 + 500 = 900$
20. $946 + 817$ → $900 + 800 = 1,700$
21. $4,284 + 6,746$ → $4,000 + 7,000 = 11,000$
22. $9,378 + 2,481$ → $9,000 + 2,000 = 11,000$
23. $6,089 + 2,784$ → $6,000 + 3,000 = 9,000$
24. $3,496 + 578$ → $3,000 + 600 = 3,600$

20   Total Problems: Total Correct: Score: © Carson-Dellosa CD-2210

Worksheet 21 — Estimating Sums

Name _____ Estimating Sums

Using the space to the right of each problem, round both numbers. Then, estimate each sum and write the answer in the space provided.

1. 82 / + 98 → 80 / +100 / 180
2. 51 / + 74 → 50 / +70 / 120
3. 28 / + 65 → 30 / +70 / 100
4. 41 / + 52 → 40 / +50 / 90
5. 486 / + 178 → 500 / +200 / 700
6. 839 / + 354 → 800 / +400 / 1,200

7. 575 / + 185 → 600 / +200 / 800
8. 618 / + 537 → 600 / +500 / 1,100
9. 386 / + 257 → 400 / +300 / 700
10. 411 / + 353 → 400 / +300 / 700
11. 914 / + 807 → 900 / +800 / 1,700
12. 752 / + 693 → 800 / +700 / 1,500

13. 987 / + 479 → 1,000 / +500 / 1,500
14. 2,408 / + 1,375 → 2,000 / +1,000 / 3,000
15. 3,993 / + 5,651 → 4,000 / +6,000 / 10,000
16. 4,197 / + 8,214 → 4,000 / +8,000 / 12,000
17. 5,312 / + 4,960 → 5,000 / +5,000 / 10,000
18. 6,153 / + 3,821 → 6,000 / +4,000 / 10,000

19. 7,252 / +2,781 → 7,000 / +3,000 / 10,000
20. 8,517 / + 5,670 → 9,000 / +6,000 / 15,000
21. 38,974 / + 25,162 → 40,000 / +30,000 / 70,000
22. 53,794 / + 52,759 → 50,000 / +50,000 / 100,000
23. 47,997 / + 41,258 → 50,000 / +40,000 / 90,000
24. 63,983 / + 29,171 → 60,000 / +30,000 / 90,000

© Carson-Dellosa CD-2210   Total Problems: ___ Total Correct: ___ Score: ___   **21**

Worksheet 22 — Problem Solving with Addition

Name _____ Problem Solving with Addition

Solve the word problems. Show your work and write the answers in the space provided.

1. Andre collected 19 rocks on the first day of the hike. On the second day, he collected 23. On the third day, he found 14 more. How many did he collect in all?

   19 / 23 / + 14 / 56

2. Robin sold 145 bars of candy the first week of the fund-raiser. The second week she sold 207. How many candy bars did she sell in all?

   145 / + 207 / 352

3. During April, Juanita sold fresh flowers at her mother's flower stand. She sold 31 dozen flowers the first week, 27 dozen the second week, 19 dozen the third week, and 14 dozen the fourth week. How many dozens of flowers did she sell during April?

   31 / 27 / 19 / + 14 / 91

4. Nadine drove 284 miles one day and 374 the next. Estimate how many miles she drove in all.

   300 / + 400 / 700

5. Keela saw 325 different cars on Friday and 287 different cars on Saturday. How many different cars did she see in all?

   325 / + 287 / 612

6. Jason picked 1,486 strawberries at his grandparents' farm one week. He picked 288 strawberries each week for two more weeks. How many did he pick in all?

   1,486 / 288 / + 288 / 2,062

22   Total Problems: ___ Total Correct: ___ Score: ___   © Carson-Dellosa CD-2210

Worksheet 23 — Basic Subtraction Facts

Name _____ Basic Subtraction Facts

Subtract. Write the answers on the lines provided.

1. 8 − 6 = 2
2. 10 − 8 = 2
3. 7 − 4 = 3
4. 9 − 3 = 6
5. 8 − 3 = 5
6. 6 − 3 = 3
7. 3 − 1 = 2
8. 4 − 3 = 1
9. 11 − 5 = 6
10. 12 − 6 = 6
11. 16 − 8 = 8
12. 13 − 6 = 7

13. 15 − 5 = 10
14. 14 − 8 = 6
15. 9 − 6 = 3
16. 18 − 9 = 9
17. 17 − 8 = 9
18. 14 − 9 = 5
19. 20 − 10 = 10
20. 14 − 6 = 8
21. 18 − 7 = 11
22. 16 − 6 = 10
23. 10 − 5 = 5
24. 12 − 2 = 10

25. 10 − 3 = 7
26. 20 − 11 = 9
27. 17 − 5 = 12
28. 18 − 6 = 12
29. 14 − 7 = 7
30. 11 − 2 = 9
31. 8 − 4 = 4
32. 12 − 4 = 8
33. 13 − 9 = 4
34. 17 − 7 = 10
35. 21 − 11 = 10
36. 24 − 12 = 12

© Carson-Dellosa CD-2210   Total Problems: ___ Total Correct: ___ Score: ___   **23**

Worksheet 24 — Subtraction without Regrouping

Name _____ Subtraction without Regrouping

Study the box below. Subtract each problem without regrouping. Then, write the answer in the space provided.

Rule:
1. Subtract the ones column.
2. Subtract the tens column.
3. Subtract the hundreds column.
4. Continue to subtract each column as needed.

Example:

98,273 / − 51,152 / 1

98,273 / − 51,152 / 21

98,273 / − 51,152 / 121

98,273 / − 51,152 / 7,121

98,273 / − 51,152 / 47,121

1. 17 / − 6 / 11
2. 15 / − 4 / 11
3. 23 / − 12 / 11
4. 17 / − 10 / 7
5. 38 / − 24 / 14

6. 46 / − 25 / 21
7. 27 / − 13 / 14
8. 42 / − 31 / 11
9. 55 / − 23 / 32
10. 67 / − 36 / 31

11. 84 / − 53 / 31
12. 75 / − 31 / 44
13. 124 / − 113 / 11
14. 342 / − 231 / 111
15. 794 / − 562 / 232

16. 478 / − 316 / 162
17. 2,568 / − 354 / 2,214
18. 4,782 / − 1,371 / 3,411
19. 2,807 / − 1,500 / 1,307
20. 9,487 / − 6,235 / 3,252

24   Total Problems: ___ Total Correct: ___ Score: ___   © Carson-Dellosa CD-2210

Subtraction with Regrouping

Name _____

Study the box below. Subtract each problem with regrouping. Then, write the answer in the space provided.

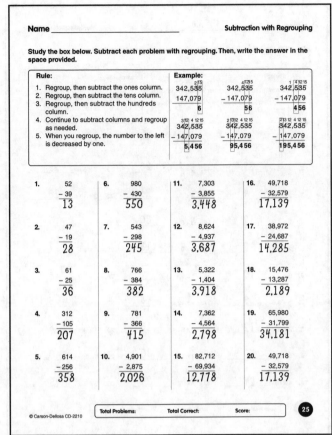

Rule:	Example:
1. Regroup, then subtract the ones column.	
2. Regroup, then subtract the tens column.	
3. Regroup, then subtract the hundreds column.	
4. Continue to subtract columns and regroup as needed.	
5. When you regroup, the number to the left is decreased by one.	

1.	52 − 39 **13**	6.	980 − 430 **550**	11.	7,303 − 3,855 **3,448**	16.	49,718 − 32,579 **17,139**
2.	47 − 19 **28**	7.	543 − 298 **245**	12.	8,624 − 4,937 **3,687**	17.	38,972 − 24,687 **14,285**
3.	61 − 25 **36**	8.	766 − 384 **382**	13.	5,322 − 1,404 **3,918**	18.	15,476 − 13,287 **2,189**
4.	312 − 105 **207**	9.	781 − 366 **415**	14.	7,362 − 4,564 **2,798**	19.	65,980 − 31,799 **34,181**
5.	614 − 256 **358**	10.	4,901 − 2,875 **2,026**	15.	82,712 − 69,934 **12,778**	20.	49,718 − 32,579 **17,139**

Total Problems: _____ Total Correct: _____ Score: _____ **25**

© Carson-Dellosa CD-2210

Subtracting with Zero

Name _____

Study the box below. Subtract and write the answer in the space provided.

Rule:	Example:
Begin subtracting in the ones place value position. When there are not enough ones from which to subtract, regroup tens. When there are not enough tens, regroup hundreds, and so on, as needed.	200 − 34 **166**

1.	40 − 19 **21**	6.	200 − 165 **35**	11.	500 − 278 **222**	16.	6,000 − 4,829 **1,171**
2.	30 − 15 **15**	7.	270 − 136 **134**	12.	700 − 484 **216**	17.	4,500 − 3,271 **1,229**
3.	70 − 24 **46**	8.	400 − 320 **80**	13.	1,000 − 256 **744**	18.	9,000 − 7,358 **1,642**
4.	150 − 36 **114**	9.	300 − 134 **166**	14.	2,500 − 1,387 **1,113**	19.	10,000 − 8,462 **1,538**
5.	250 − 33 **217**	10.	800 − 522 **278**	15.	7,000 − 3,572 **3,428**	20.	10,000 − 9,897 **103**

26 Total Problems: _____ Total Correct: _____ Score: _____

© Carson-Dellosa CD-2210

Subtracting Large Numbers

Name _____

Answer each problem in the space provided. Use regrouping as needed.

1.	496 − 237 **259**	7.	1,800 − 539 **1,261**	13.	79,136 − 5,564 **73,572**	19.	300,000 − 273,189 **26,811**
2.	742 − 429 **313**	8.	28,362 − 14,795 **13,567**	14.	97,612 − 46,378 **51,234**	20.	465,238 − 254,189 **211,049**
3.	643 − 286 **357**	9.	34,607 − 25,350 **9,257**	15.	42,320 − 41,412 **908**	21.	489,284 − 232,422 **256,862**
4.	828 − 537 **291**	10.	24,816 − 18,912 **5,904**	16.	88,177 − 66,250 **21,927**	22.	1,777,333 − 455,999 **1,321,334**
5.	726 − 618 **108**	11.	45,324 − 41,188 **4,136**	17.	120,436 − 75,328 **45,108**	23.	906,589 − 552,978 **353,611**
6.	1,398 − 852 **546**	12.	50,000 − 31,217 **18,783**	18.	250,000 − 175,000 **75,000**	24.	2,001,551 − 987,845 **1,013,706**

Total Problems: _____ Total Correct: _____ Score: _____ **27**

© Carson-Dellosa CD-2210

Subtraction Practice

Name _____

Answer each problem in the space provided.

1.	35 − 9 **26**	8.	700 − 522 **178**	15.	96,132 − 37,488 **58,644**	22.	305,061 − 184,235 **120,826**
2.	72 − 40 **32**	9.	350 − 207 **143**	16.	93,246 − 75,369 **17,877**	23.	704,188 − 96,256 **607,932**
3.	184 − 69 **115**	10.	7,521 − 3,488 **4,033**	17.	100,000 − 54,000 **46,000**	24.	846,137 − 278,429 **567,708**
4.	136 − 78 **58**	11.	10,892 − 7,468 **3,424**	18.	105,111 − 63,999 **41,112**	25.	600,000 − 159,744 **440,256**
5.	257 − 34 **223**	12.	9,464 − 3,597 **5,867**	19.	122,555 − 77,878 **44,677**	26.	940,905 − 88,499 **852,406**
6.	521 − 356 **165**	13.	43,282 − 31,465 **11,817**	20.	155,232 − 86,456 **68,776**	27.	1,300,588 − 455,297 **845,291**
7.	688 − 309 **379**	14.	85,016 − 54,258 **30,758**	21.	200,000 − 86,555 **113,445**	28.	1,566,892 − 578,489 **988,403**

28 Total Problems: _____ Total Correct: _____ Score: _____

© Carson-Dellosa CD-2210

© Carson-Dellosa CD-2210

Problem Solving with Subtraction

Name _____

Solve the word problems. Show your work and write the answers in the space provided.

1. Delaney had 27 days to work on her science project. After working for 13 days, she was half finished. How many days did she have left to work on her project?

$$\begin{array}{r} 27 \\ -13 \\ \hline 14 \end{array}$$

2. Isaiah's father took a trip that was 396 miles long. He drove 115 miles the first day. How many miles did he have left to drive?

$$\begin{array}{r} 396 \\ -115 \\ \hline 281 \end{array}$$

3. The pet store had 648 goldfish. Employees sold 394 goldfish in one week. How many goldfish were left?

$$\begin{array}{r} 648 \\ -394 \\ \hline 254 \end{array}$$

4. Margaret collected 1,498 stickers. She gave 745 to her friends. How many did she have left?

$$\begin{array}{r} 1,498 \\ -745 \\ \hline 753 \end{array}$$

5. Tara's mother baked 72 chocolate chip cookies and 145 sugar cookies. If 89 sugar cookies were eaten, how many sugar cookies remained?

$$\begin{array}{r} 145 \\ -89 \\ \hline 56 \end{array}$$

6. Zachary's basketball team scored 800 points in their second season. In their first season, they scored 650 points. How many more points did they score in the second season?

$$\begin{array}{r} 800 \\ -650 \\ \hline 150 \end{array}$$

7. Mr. Fleming's copier made 45,862 copies in July. In August, the copier made 65,012 copies. How many more copies did it make in August?

$$\begin{array}{r} 65,012 \\ -45,862 \\ \hline 19,150 \end{array}$$

8. Jason rode his bike 372 miles in May. In June he rode 224 miles. How many more miles did he ride in May?

$$\begin{array}{r} 372 \\ -224 \\ \hline 148 \end{array}$$

Total Problems: _____ Total Correct: _____ Score: _____ **29**

© Carson-Dellosa CD-2210

Multiplication Facts 0-5

Name _____

Study the box below. Then, answer each problem on the line provided.

Rule:
0 multiplied by any number will always equal 0.
Any number multiplied by 1 will always equal that number.

Examples:
0 x 5 = 0   5 x 1 = 5
0 x 10 = 0   12 x 1 = 12
0 x 100 = 0   100 x 1 = 100

1. 0 x 2 = 0
2. 4 x 8 = 32
3. 2 x 2 = 4
4. 3 x 4 = 12
5. 2 x 1 = 2
6. 5 x 2 = 10
7. 3 x 3 = 9
8. 2 x 6 = 12
9. 5 x 8 = 40
10. 4 x 6 = 24
11. 5 x 3 = 15
12. 3 x 8 = 24
13. 3 x 7 = 21
14. 5 x 6 = 30
15. 2 x 9 = 18
16. 1 x 9 = 9
17. 4 x 12 = 48
18. 2 x 8 = 16
19. 3 x 10 = 30
20. 2 x 12 = 24
21. 0 x 4 = 0
22. 5 x 5 = 25
23. 2 x 10 = 20
24. 5 x 1 = 5
25. 3 x 9 = 27
26. 4 x 7 = 28
27. 3 x 2 = 6
28. 1 x 8 = 8
29. 0 x 3 = 0
30. 5 x 9 = 45

30 Total Problems: _____ Total Correct: _____ Score: _____

© Carson-Dellosa CD-2210

Multiplication Facts 6-9

Name _____

Study the box below. Then, solve the problems and write each answer on the line provided.

Rule:
Multiplying is just a faster way of adding.
By learning the basic facts, you can find out "how many in all" much faster.

Example: 3 x 6 = ___
3 x 6 = 3 groups of 6 things, like books
6 books + 6 books + 6 books = 18 books
3 x 6 = 18

1. 6 x 4 = 24
2. 8 x 5 = 40
3. 7 x 3 = 21
4. 8 x 8 = 64
5. 9 x 7 = 63
6. 7 x 8 = 56
7. 6 x 8 = 48
8. 7 x 10 = 70
9. 6 x 5 = 30
10. 9 x 9 = 81
11. 8 x 10 = 80
12. 8 x 4 = 32
13. 7 x 5 = 35
14. 9 x 8 = 72
15. 6 x 2 = 12
16. 8 x 6 = 48
17. 9 x 2 = 18
18. 9 x 11 = 99
19. 6 x 12 = 72
20. 9 x 3 = 27
21. 6 x 9 = 54
22. 9 x 4 = 36
23. 7 x 6 = 42
24. 7 x 9 = 63
25. 6 x 10 = 60
26. 9 x 5 = 45
27. 6 x 6 = 36
28. 7 x 7 = 49
29. 9 x 12 = 108
30. 6 x 7 = 42

© Carson-Dellosa CD-2210 Total Problems: _____ Total Correct: _____ Score: _____ **31**

Mastering Multiplication Facts

Name _____

Multiply each problem. Then, write the answer in the space provided.

1. 1 x 6 = 6
2. 3 x 7 = 21
3. 4 x 5 = 20
4. 6 x 4 = 24
5. 3 x 8 = 24
6. 2 x 7 = 14
7. 8 x 6 = 48
8. 4 x 3 = 12
9. 5 x 5 = 25
10. 6 x 5 = 30
11. 9 x 2 = 18
12. 3 x 3 = 9
13. 9 x 5 = 45
14. 8 x 7 = 56
15. 12 x 8 = 96
16. 10 x 7 = 70
17. 5 x 2 = 10
18. 9 x 3 = 27
19. 12 x 2 = 24
20. 12 x 3 = 36
21. 8 x 9 = 72
22. 5 x 7 = 35
23. 11 x 5 = 55
24. 11 x 9 = 99
25. 10 x 3 = 30
26. 4 x 9 = 36
27. 11 x 4 = 44
28. 10 x 4 = 40
29. 10 x 5 = 50
30. 11 x 7 = 77
31. 12 x 9 = 108
32. 11 x 8 = 88

32 Total Problems: _____ Total Correct: _____ Score: _____

© Carson-Dellosa CD-2210

© Carson-Dellosa CD-2210

Worksheet 33 — Multiplying One- and Two-Digit Numbers

Name _____

Study the box below. Then, solve each problem. Write the answer in the space provided.

Rule:	Example:
Multiply ones, then regroup.	$\overset{1}{23}$ $\overset{1}{23}$
Multiply tens, then add extra tens.	$\times\ 6$ $\times\ 6$
	8 138

1. 10 × 5 = **50**
2. 10 × 3 = **30**
3. 12 × 2 = **24**
4. 11 × 3 = **33**
5. 13 × 5 = **65**
6. 10 × 4 = **40**

7. 15 × 4 = **60**
8. 19 × 2 = **38**
9. 31 × 4 = **124**
10. 48 × 3 = **144**
11. 30 × 6 = **180**
12. 24 × 5 = **120**

13. 62 × 2 = **124**
14. 27 × 3 = **81**
15. 54 × 3 = **162**
16. 73 × 3 = **219**
17. 97 × 3 = **291**
18. 80 × 4 = **320**

19. 79 × 3 = **237**
20. 87 × 5 = **435**
21. 90 × 4 = **360**
22. 82 × 9 = **738**
23. 94 × 7 = **658**
24. 98 × 6 = **588**

Total Problems: Total Correct: Score:

33

Worksheet 34 — Multiplying One- and Three-Digit Numbers

Name _____

Study the box below. Then, solve each problem. Write the answer in the space provided.

Rule:	Example:
1. Multiply ones, then regroup.	423 423 423
2. Multiply tens, then add extra tens.	$\times\ 2$ $\times\ 2$ $\times\ 2$
3. Multiply hundreds.	6 46 846
4. Regroup as needed.	

1. 100 × 3 = **300**
2. 120 × 2 = **240**
3. 300 × 5 = **1,500**
4. 250 × 4 = **1,000**
5. 145 × 2 = **290**

6. 278 × 4 = **1,112**
7. 329 × 3 = **987**
8. 640 × 5 = **3,200**
9. 710 × 6 = **4,260**
10. 518 × 7 = **3,626**

11. 422 × 5 = **2,110**
12. 705 × 4 = **2,820**
13. 826 × 8 = **6,608**
14. 900 × 3 = **2,700**
15. 715 × 6 = **4,290**

16. 827 × 9 = **7,443**
17. 926 × 7 = **6,482**
18. 686 × 8 = **5,488**
19. 912 × 3 = **2,736**
20. 847 × 5 = **4,235**

34   Total Problems: Total Correct: Score:

Worksheet 35 — Multiplying Two- and Three-Digit Numbers

Name _____

Study the box below. Then, solve each problem. Write the answer in the space provided.

Rule:	Example:
1. Multiply ones by ones, tens, and hundreds. Regroup as needed.	325 325 325
2. Multiply tens by ones, tens, and hundreds. Regroup as needed.	$\times\ 43$ $\times\ 43$ $\times\ 43$
3. Add the two numbers to find the final product.	975 975 975
	1,300 +1,300
	13,975

1. 203 × 12 = **2,436**
2. 370 × 15 = **5,550**
3. 150 × 21 = **3,150**

4. 330 × 25 = **8,250**
5. 451 × 36 = **16,236**
6. 522 × 40 = **20,880**

7. 633 × 61 = **38,613**
8. 357 × 51 = **18,207**
9. 278 × 55 = **15,290**

10. 567 × 38 = **21,546**
11. 629 × 88 = **55,352**
12. 783 × 52 = **40,716**

Total Problems: Total Correct: Score:

35

Worksheet 36 — Multiplication Rounding and Estimating

Name _____

Study the box below. Round the two-digit factor and leave the one-digit factor as is. Multiply to find the estimated product. Then, write the answer in the space provided.

Rule:	Example:
Since it is easier to multiply by numbers ending in 0, it can be useful to estimate an approximate answer by rounding.	26 × 9 = ____
	26 rounds up to **30**, so the estimated product is:
	30 × 9 = **270**

1. 18 → 20 × 2 = **40**
2. 23 → 20 × 5 = **100**
3. 15 → 20 × 3 = **60**
4. 33 → 30 × 6 = **180**
5. 46 → 50 × 4 = **200**

6. 24 → 20 × 9 = **180**
7. 58 → 60 × 5 = **300**
8. 64 → 60 × 7 = **420**
9. 72 → 70 × 2 = **140**
10. 53 → 50 × 6 = **300**

11. 75 → 80 × 4 = **320**
12. 81 → 80 × 8 = **640**
13. 94 → 90 × 5 = **450**
14. 70 → 70 × 3 = **210**
15. 98 → 100 × 6 = **600**

36   Total Problems: Total Correct: Score:

85

Worksheet 37 (top left)

Name _____ **Estimating Products with Multiplication**

Study the examples below. Round each factor to the greatest place value represented. Then, multiply to find the estimated product. Write the answer in the space provided.

Examples:

325	rounds to	300	5,928	rounds to	6,000
x 29	rounds to	x 30	x 12	rounds to	x 10
		9,000			**60,000**

1. 24 20
   x31 x 30
       600

2. 37 40
   x26 x 30
       1,200

3. 50 50
   x35 x 40
       2,000

4. 78 80
   x64 x 60
       4,800

5. 89 90
   x29 x 30
       2,700

6. 134 100
   x20 x 20
       2,000

7. 188 200
   x43 x 40
       8,000

8. 205 200
   x29 x 30
       6,000

9. 278 300
   x41 x 40
       12,000

10. 327 300
    x56 x 60
        18,000

11. 415 400
    x92 x 90
        36,000

12. 675 700
    x85 x 90
        63,000

13. 563 600
    x47 x 50
        30,000

14. 917 900
    x39 x 40
        36,000

15. 1,000 1,000
    x25 x 30
        30,000

16. 1,254 1,000
    x36 x 40
        40,000

© Carson-Dellosa CD-2210

Total Problems: _____ Total Correct: _____ Score: _____ **37**

Worksheet 38 (top right)

Name _____ **Problem Solving with Multiplication**

Solve the word problems. Show your work and write the answers in the space provided.

1. Sophia's Bakery sold 8 cakes each day for 21 days. How many cakes did the bakery sell in all?

   21
   x 8
   168

2. For 21 days of camp, Melanie collected 2 souvenirs each day. How many souvenirs did she collect in all?

   21
   x 2
   42

3. Matt planted 25 fruit trees each day for 18 days. How many fruit trees did he plant in all?

   25
   x 18
   450

4. Mr. Sanders ordered 56 boxes of videotapes for his store. Each box had 35 tapes. How many videotapes did he receive in all?

   56
   x 35
   1,960

5. Regina made 49 gift baskets each week for 5 weeks. Estimate how many gift baskets she made.

   50
   x 5
   250

6. Donna sold 136 bags of popcorn at the movie theater for 24 days. Estimate to find out about how many bags of popcorn Donna sold.

   140
   x 20
   2,800

7. Jerome practiced with his soccer team 4 hours each day for 159 days. How many hours in all did Jerome practice?

   159
   x 4
   636

8. Christina has collected 156 unusual coins every year for 18 years. How many coins has she collected in all?

   156
   x 18
   2,808

38 Total Problems: _____ Total Correct: _____ Score: _____ © Carson-Dellosa CD-2210

Worksheet 39 (bottom left)

Name _____ **Division Facts 0-1**

Study the box below. Solve each problem. Then, write the answer on the line provided.

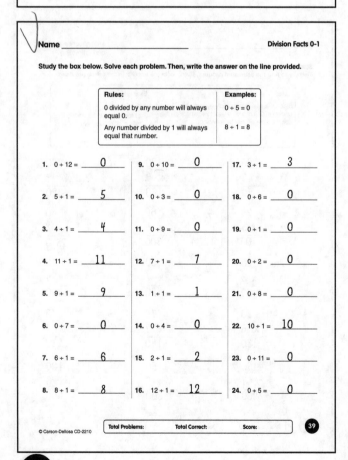

Rules:	**Examples:**
0 divided by any number will always equal 0.	0 ÷ 5 = 0
Any number divided by 1 will always equal that number.	8 ÷ 1 = 8

1. 0 ÷ 12 = **0**
2. 5 ÷ 1 = **5**
3. 4 ÷ 1 = **4**
4. 11 ÷ 1 = **11**
5. 9 ÷ 1 = **9**
6. 0 ÷ 7 = **0**
7. 6 ÷ 1 = **6**
8. 8 ÷ 1 = **8**

9. 0 ÷ 10 = **0**
10. 0 ÷ 3 = **0**
11. 0 ÷ 9 = **0**
12. 7 ÷ 1 = **7**
13. 1 ÷ 1 = **1**
14. 0 ÷ 4 = **0**
15. 2 ÷ 1 = **2**
16. 12 ÷ 1 = **12**

17. 3 ÷ 1 = **3**
18. 0 ÷ 6 = **0**
19. 0 ÷ 1 = **0**
20. 0 ÷ 2 = **0**
21. 0 ÷ 8 = **0**
22. 10 ÷ 1 = **10**
23. 0 ÷ 11 = **0**
24. 0 ÷ 5 = **0**

© Carson-Dellosa CD-2210

Total Problems: _____ Total Correct: _____ Score: _____ **39**

Worksheet 40 (bottom right)

Name _____ **Division Facts 2-4**

Study the box below. Solve each problem. Then, write the answer on the line provided.

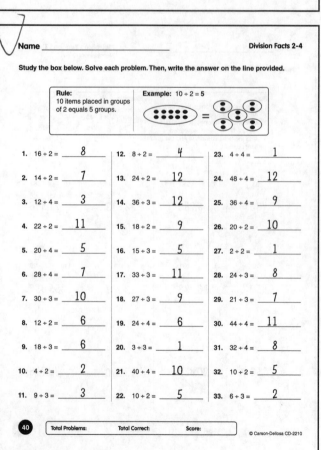

Rule:	**Example:** 10 ÷ 2 = 5
10 items placed in groups of 2 equals 5 groups.	

1. 16 ÷ 2 = **8**
2. 14 ÷ 2 = **7**
3. 12 ÷ 4 = **3**
4. 22 ÷ 2 = **11**
5. 20 ÷ 4 = **5**
6. 28 ÷ 4 = **7**
7. 30 ÷ 3 = **10**
8. 12 ÷ 2 = **6**
9. 18 ÷ 3 = **6**
10. 4 ÷ 2 = **2**
11. 9 ÷ 3 = **3**

12. 8 ÷ 2 = **4**
13. 24 ÷ 2 = **12**
14. 36 ÷ 3 = **12**
15. 18 ÷ 2 = **9**
16. 15 ÷ 3 = **5**
17. 33 ÷ 3 = **11**
18. 27 ÷ 3 = **9**
19. 24 ÷ 4 = **6**
20. 3 ÷ 3 = **1**
21. 40 ÷ 4 = **10**
22. 10 ÷ 2 = **5**

23. 4 ÷ 4 = **1**
24. 48 ÷ 4 = **12**
25. 36 ÷ 4 = **9**
26. 20 ÷ 2 = **10**
27. 2 ÷ 2 = **1**
28. 24 ÷ 3 = **8**
29. 21 ÷ 3 = **7**
30. 44 ÷ 4 = **11**
31. 32 ÷ 4 = **8**
32. 10 ÷ 2 = **5**
33. 6 ÷ 3 = **2**

40 Total Problems: _____ Total Correct: _____ Score: _____ © Carson-Dellosa CD-2210

Worksheet 41 — Division Facts 5-7

Name _____   Division Facts 5-7

Solve each problem. Then, write the answer on the line provided.

1. $30 \div 5 =$ __6__
2. $12 \div 6 =$ __2__
3. $40 \div 5 =$ __8__
4. $18 \div 6 =$ __3__
5. $42 \div 6 =$ __7__
6. $35 \div 7 =$ __5__
7. $48 \div 6 =$ __8__
8. $20 \div 5 =$ __4__
9. $56 \div 7 =$ __8__
10. $54 \div 6 =$ __9__
11. $15 \div 5 =$ __3__
12. $28 \div 7 =$ __4__
13. $70 \div 7 =$ __10__
14. $63 \div 7 =$ __9__
15. $7 \div 7 =$ __1__
16. $36 \div 6 =$ __6__
17. $55 \div 5 =$ __11__
18. $45 \div 5 =$ __9__
19. $49 \div 7 =$ __7__
20. $60 \div 6 =$ __10__
21. $25 \div 5 =$ __5__
22. $60 \div 5 =$ __12__
23. $77 \div 7 =$ __11__
24. $14 \div 7 =$ __2__
25. $10 \div 5 =$ __2__
26. $84 \div 7 =$ __12__
27. $66 \div 6 =$ __11__

Total Problems: ____ Total Correct: ____ Score: ____ 41

© Carson-Dellosa CD-2210

Worksheet 42 — Division Facts 8-9

Name _____   Division Facts 8-9

Solve each problem. Write the answer on the line provided.

1. $16 \div 8 =$ __2__
2. $36 \div 9 =$ __4__
3. $88 \div 8 =$ __11__
4. $45 \div 9 =$ __5__
5. $27 \div 9 =$ __3__
6. $40 \div 8 =$ __5__
7. $8 \div 8 =$ __1__
8. $48 \div 8 =$ __6__
9. $24 \div 8 =$ __3__
10. $72 \div 9 =$ __8__
11. $32 \div 8 =$ __4__
12. $81 \div 9 =$ __9__
13. $90 \div 9 =$ __10__
14. $64 \div 8 =$ __8__
15. $18 \div 9 =$ __2__
16. $9 \div 9 =$ __1__
17. $54 \div 9 =$ __6__
18. $56 \div 8 =$ __7__
19. $72 \div 8 =$ __9__
20. $80 \div 8 =$ __10__
21. $96 \div 8 =$ __12__
22. $63 \div 9 =$ __7__
23. $108 \div 9 =$ __12__
24. $99 \div 9 =$ __11__

42 Total Problems: ____ Total Correct: ____ Score: ____

© Carson-Dellosa CD-2210

Worksheet 43 — Division Mixed Practice

Name _____   Division Mixed Practice

Study the example below. Solve each problem. Then, write the answer in the space provided.

Example:
$$6\overline{)30}$$ = 5
Think: 6 divides evenly into 30, leaving no remainder.

1. $5\overline{)30}$ = 6
2. $3\overline{)18}$ = 6
3. $8\overline{)8}$ = 1
4. $4\overline{)32}$ = 8
5. $7\overline{)14}$ = 2
6. $8\overline{)56}$ = 7
7. $6\overline{)36}$ = 6
8. $1\overline{)4}$ = 4
9. $4\overline{)28}$ = 7
10. $3\overline{)33}$ = 11
11. $2\overline{)8}$ = 4
12. $8\overline{)40}$ = 5
13. $3\overline{)24}$ = 8
14. $8\overline{)64}$ = 8
15. $9\overline{)81}$ = 9
16. $2\overline{)18}$ = 9

Total Problems: ____ Total Correct: ____ Score: ____ 43

© Carson-Dellosa CD-2210

Worksheet 44 — Division with No Remainders

Name _____   Division with No Remainders

Study the example below. Then, solve each problem. Show your work and write the answer in the space provided.

Example:
$$
\begin{array}{r}
12 \\
4\overline{)48} \\
-4 \\
\hline
08 \\
-8 \\
\hline
0
\end{array}
$$
Think: 4 divides evenly into 48, leaving no remainder.

1. $2\overline{)64}$ = 32
2. $3\overline{)69}$ = 23
3. $4\overline{)32}$ = 8
4. $9\overline{)90}$ = 10
5. $3\overline{)36}$ = 12
6. $4\overline{)84}$ = 21
7. $6\overline{)72}$ = 12
8. $6\overline{)84}$ = 14
9. $2\overline{)98}$ = 49
10. $4\overline{)100}$ = 25
11. $5\overline{)125}$ = 25
12. $3\overline{)123}$ = 41

44 Total Problems: ____ Total Correct: ____ Score: ____

© Carson-Dellosa CD-2210

Worksheet 45 — Division with Remainders

Name _____   **Division with Remainders**

Study the example below. Then, solve each problem. Show your work and write the answer in the space provided.

Example:

$$\begin{array}{r} 8\ R3 \\ 4\overline{)35} \\ -32 \\ \hline 3 \end{array}$$

Think:
35 divided by 4 is **8** because 8 x 4 is closest to 35 without exceeding 35.

Then, 35 − 32 is 3, and **3** is called the remainder.

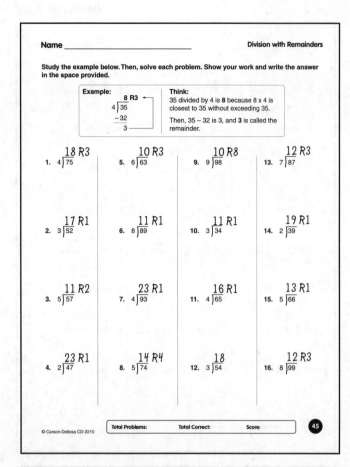

1. $4\overline{)75}$ → 18 R3
5. $6\overline{)63}$ → 10 R3
9. $9\overline{)98}$ → 10 R8
13. $7\overline{)87}$ → 12 R3

2. $3\overline{)52}$ → 17 R1
6. $8\overline{)89}$ → 11 R1
10. $3\overline{)34}$ → 11 R1
14. $2\overline{)39}$ → 19 R1

3. $5\overline{)57}$ → 11 R2
7. $4\overline{)93}$ → 23 R1
11. $4\overline{)65}$ → 16 R1
15. $5\overline{)66}$ → 13 R1

4. $2\overline{)47}$ → 23 R1
8. $5\overline{)74}$ → 14 R4
12. $3\overline{)54}$ → 18
16. $8\overline{)99}$ → 12 R3

Total Problems: Total Correct: Score: **45**

© Carson-Dellosa CD-2210

Worksheet 46 — Estimating Quotients

Name _____   **Estimating Quotients**

Study the example below. Then, estimate the quotient for each problem. Show your work and write the answer in the space provided.

Example: $4\overline{)62}$

Round 62 to the nearest 10. $4\overline{)60}$

$$\begin{array}{r} 15 \\ 4\overline{)60} \\ -4 \\ \hline 20 \\ -20 \\ \hline 0 \end{array}$$

Then, divide as usual.

Therefore, the estimated quotient is **15**.

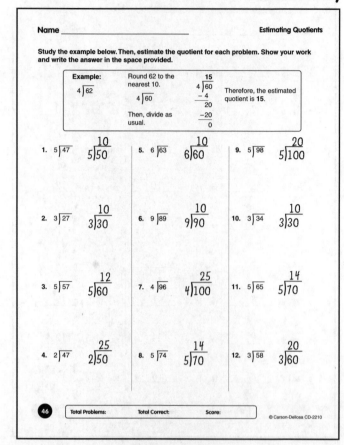

1. $5\overline{)47}$ → $5\overline{)50}$ = 10
5. $6\overline{)63}$ → $6\overline{)60}$ = 10
9. $5\overline{)98}$ → $5\overline{)100}$ = 20

2. $3\overline{)27}$ → $3\overline{)30}$ = 10
6. $9\overline{)89}$ → $9\overline{)90}$ = 10
10. $3\overline{)34}$ → $3\overline{)30}$ = 10

3. $5\overline{)57}$ → $5\overline{)60}$ = 12
7. $4\overline{)96}$ → $4\overline{)100}$ = 25
11. $5\overline{)65}$ → $5\overline{)70}$ = 14

4. $2\overline{)47}$ → $2\overline{)50}$ = 25
8. $5\overline{)74}$ → $5\overline{)70}$ = 14
12. $3\overline{)58}$ → $3\overline{)60}$ = 20

46   Total Problems: Total Correct: Score:

© Carson-Dellosa CD-2210

Worksheet 47 — Problem Solving with Division

Name _____   **Problem Solving with Division**

Solve the word problems. Show your work and write the answers in the space provided.

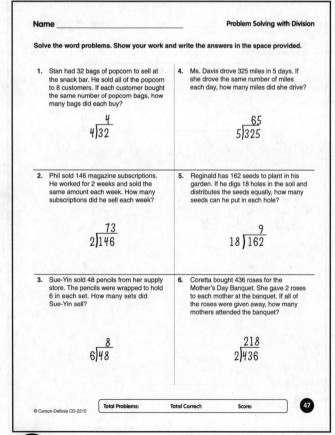

1. Stan had 32 bags of popcorn to sell at the snack bar. He sold all of the popcorn to 8 customers. If each customer bought the same number of popcorn bags, how many bags did each buy?

$$4\overline{)32} = 4$$

2. Phil sold 146 magazine subscriptions. He worked for 2 weeks and sold the same amount each week. How many subscriptions did he sell each week?

$$2\overline{)146} = 73$$

3. Sue-Yin sold 48 pencils from her supply store. The pencils were wrapped to hold 6 in each set. How many sets did Sue-Yin sell?

$$6\overline{)48} = 8$$

4. Ms. Davis drove 325 miles in 5 days. If she drove the same number of miles each day, how many miles did she drive?

$$5\overline{)325} = 65$$

5. Reginald has 162 seeds to plant in his garden. If he digs 18 holes in the soil and distributes the seeds equally, how many seeds can he put in each hole?

$$18\overline{)162} = 9$$

6. Coretta bought 436 roses for the Mother's Day Banquet. She gave 2 roses to each mother at the banquet. If all of the roses were given away, how many mothers attended the banquet?

$$2\overline{)436} = 218$$

Total Problems: Total Correct: Score: **47**

© Carson-Dellosa CD-2210

Worksheet 48 — Parts of a Whole

Name _____   **Parts of a Whole**

Study the example below. Circle the fraction which names the shaded part of each figure.

Example:

Think:
A fraction names a part of the whole. Since 1 out of 2 parts of the circle is shaded, $\frac{1}{2}$ names the shaded part.

$\frac{1}{2}$ $\frac{1}{3}$ $\frac{1}{4}$

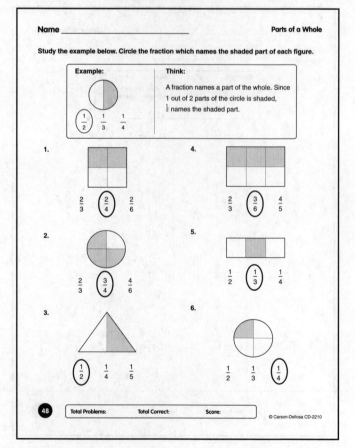

1. $\frac{2}{3}$ $\boxed{\frac{2}{4}}$ $\frac{2}{6}$

2. $\frac{2}{3}$ $\boxed{\frac{3}{4}}$ $\frac{4}{6}$

3. $\boxed{\frac{1}{2}}$ $\frac{1}{4}$ $\frac{1}{5}$

4. $\frac{2}{3}$ $\boxed{\frac{3}{6}}$ $\frac{4}{5}$

5. $\frac{1}{2}$ $\boxed{\frac{1}{3}}$ $\frac{1}{4}$

6. $\frac{1}{2}$ $\frac{1}{3}$ $\boxed{\frac{1}{4}}$

48   Total Problems: Total Correct: Score:

© Carson-Dellosa CD-2210

Name _____   Parts of a Group

Study the box below. Determine the correct fraction for each problem. Then, write the answer on the line provided.

Rule:	Example:
To determine a fraction for parts of a group, first find the total number of items in the group. This total will always be the denominator, the number that is on the bottom.	Stacy has 20 students in her class. There are 11 girls and 9 boys. What fraction of the class is boys? **Answer:** $\frac{9}{20}$ There are 20 students, and 9 out of 20 are boys.

1. Stuart has a vegetable garden growing in his yard. From it he picked the following vegetables: 3 tomatoes, 4 cucumbers, 5 zucchini, 3 squash, 2 peppers, and 3 carrots. Write the fraction of each vegetable he picked.

    A.   tomatoes $\frac{3}{20}$ D.   squash $\frac{3}{20}$

    B.   cucumbers $\frac{4}{20}$ E.   peppers $\frac{2}{20}$

    C.   zucchini $\frac{5}{20}$ F.   carrots $\frac{3}{20}$

2. Juan opened his bag of multi-colored candy, dumped it on the table, and counted how many pieces of each color he had. He counted 12 blue pieces, 14 red, 8 orange, 6 green, 9 yellow, and 5 brown. Write the fraction of each color he counted.

    A.   blue $\frac{12}{54}$ D.   green $\frac{6}{54}$

    B.   red $\frac{14}{54}$ E.   yellow $\frac{9}{54}$

    C.   orange $\frac{8}{54}$ F.   brown $\frac{5}{54}$

3. Mrs. King has just finished sorting the books in her class library. She has 35 fiction and 28 nonfiction books. Write the fraction of each type of book.

    A.   fiction $\frac{35}{63}$ B.   nonfiction $\frac{28}{63}$

Total Problems:	Total Correct:	Score:	**49**

Name _____   Comparing Fractions

Study the box below. Then, compare the fractions using <, >, or =. In the square provided, place the symbol that would make each number sentence true.

Rules:	Examples:
When comparing two fractions with the same denominator, compare their numerators, the numbers that are on top. When comparing fractions that have different denominators, it may help to draw a diagram to compare them.	6 is greater than 4 $\frac{6}{10}$ **>** $\frac{4}{10}$ $\frac{1}{3}$ **<** $\frac{3}{6}$

1. $\frac{2}{3}$ **>** $\frac{1}{3}$ 6. $\frac{12}{13}$ **>** $\frac{11}{13}$ 11. $\frac{1}{12}$ **<** $\frac{1}{3}$

2. $\frac{5}{9}$ **<** $\frac{6}{9}$ 7. $\frac{2}{6}$ **<** $\frac{3}{6}$ 12. $\frac{1}{5}$ **<** $\frac{7}{10}$

3. $\frac{10}{12}$ **=** $\frac{10}{12}$ 8. $\frac{5}{7}$ **<** $\frac{6}{7}$ 13. $\frac{1}{4}$ **>** $\frac{1}{8}$

4. $\frac{1}{4}$ **<** $\frac{2}{4}$ 9. $\frac{6}{8}$ **<** $\frac{7}{8}$ 14. $\frac{1}{5}$ **=** $\frac{1}{5}$

5. $\frac{2}{5}$ **<** $\frac{4}{5}$ 10. $\frac{1}{3}$ **>** $\frac{1}{6}$ 15. $\frac{1}{6}$ **>** $\frac{1}{8}$

50	Total Problems:	Total Correct:	Score:	

Name _____   Fractional Parts

Study the box below. Then, solve each problem. Write the answer in the space provided.

Rules:	Examples:
To find $\frac{1}{2}$ of a number, divide by 2.	$\frac{1}{2}$ of 12 is **6**
To find $\frac{1}{3}$ of a number, divide by 3.	$\frac{1}{3}$ of 12 is **4**
To find $\frac{1}{4}$ of a number, divide by 4.	$\frac{1}{4}$ of 12 is **3**

1. $\frac{1}{2}$ of 10 = 5   5. $\frac{1}{3}$ of 9 = 3   9. $\frac{1}{4}$ of 16 = 4

2. $\frac{1}{3}$ of 15 = 5   6. $\frac{1}{5}$ of 25 = 5   10. $\frac{1}{7}$ of 14 = 2

3. $\frac{1}{2}$ of 30 = 15   7. $\frac{1}{2}$ of 18 = 9   11. $\frac{1}{5}$ of 20 = 4

4. $\frac{1}{4}$ of 8 = 2   8. $\frac{1}{6}$ of 24 = 4   12. $\frac{1}{8}$ of 48 = 6

Total Problems:	Total Correct:	Score:	**51**

Name _____   Adding and Subtracting Fractions

Study the box below. Then, solve each problem. Write the answer in the space provided. Pay careful attention to the sign.

Rule:	Examples:
When adding or subtracting fractions with the same denominator: First, add or subtract their numerators. Then, write that number over the same denominator.	$\frac{3}{8} + \frac{2}{8} = \frac{5}{8}$ $\frac{9}{10} - \frac{3}{10} = \frac{6}{10}$

1. $\frac{4}{7} - \frac{2}{7} = \frac{2}{7}$ 6. $\frac{1}{3} + \frac{1}{3} = \frac{2}{3}$ 11. $\frac{7}{8} - \frac{5}{8} = \frac{2}{8}$

2. $\frac{3}{11} + \frac{5}{11} = \frac{8}{11}$ 7. $\frac{10}{25} - \frac{3}{25} = \frac{7}{25}$ 12. $\frac{1}{5} - \frac{1}{5} = 0$

3. $\frac{9}{14} - \frac{8}{14} = \frac{1}{14}$ 8. $\frac{1}{4} + \frac{2}{4} = \frac{3}{4}$ 13. $\frac{5}{15} - \frac{1}{15} = \frac{4}{15}$

4. $\frac{3}{20} + \frac{4}{20} = \frac{7}{20}$ 9. $\frac{7}{12} - \frac{2}{12} = \frac{5}{12}$ 14. $\frac{1}{10} + \frac{3}{10} = \frac{4}{10}$

5. $\frac{4}{5} - \frac{3}{5} = \frac{1}{5}$ 10. $\frac{5}{16} + \frac{4}{16} = \frac{9}{16}$ 15. $\frac{9}{15} - \frac{4}{15} = \frac{5}{15}$

52	Total Problems:	Total Correct:	Score:	

89

Worksheet 53 — Problem Solving with Fractions

Name _____ Problem Solving with Fractions

Solve the word problems. Show your work and write the answers in the space provided.

1. Marissa cut her apple pie into eighths, and she served 5 pieces to her guests for dessert. Did she serve more or less than half the pie?

$$\frac{5}{8} > \frac{1}{2} \quad \text{(more)}$$

2. Jake ordered a pizza and asked for it to be cut into sixths. Maurice also ordered a pizza, but he asked for it to be cut into eighths. Who had larger pieces?

$$\frac{1}{6} > \frac{1}{8} \quad \text{(Jake)}$$

3. Each child received $\frac{1}{3}$ of the 15 marbles needed to play a game. How many did each child receive?

$$\frac{1}{3} \text{ of } 15 = 5$$

4. Cara had 10 pieces of paper. She used 2 in math class and 3 in English. What fraction of paper did she use?

$$\frac{5}{10} \text{ or } \frac{1}{2}$$

5. There are 24 students in Martel's class. Half of them are boys. How many boys are in his class?

$$\frac{1}{2} \text{ of } 24 = 12$$

6. David has 30 shirts in his closet. One-third of them have long sleeves. How many long-sleeved shirts does he have?

$$\frac{1}{3} \text{ of } 30 = 10$$

7. Reese cut the pan of brownies into eighths. He ate $\frac{3}{8}$ of the pan, and his friend ate $\frac{2}{8}$. What fraction of the brownies did they eat in all? What fraction was left over?

$$\frac{3}{8} + \frac{2}{8} = \frac{5}{8}; \quad \frac{8}{8} - \frac{5}{8} = \frac{3}{8}$$

8. Brent's Automotive Store sold $\frac{2}{5}$ of its tires on Monday and $\frac{1}{5}$ of its tires on Tuesday. What fraction of tires were sold?

$$\frac{2}{5} + \frac{1}{5} = \frac{3}{5}$$

© Carson-Dellosa CD-2210   Total Problems: Total Correct: Score: **53**

Worksheet 54 — Decimal Place Value

Name _____ Decimal Place Value

Study the box below. Then, follow the directions.

Rule:	Example:
The decimal point separates the ones digit from the tenths digit.	21.45 =

2	1	.4	5
tens	ones	tenths	hundredths

Underline the digit in the tenths place.

1. 38.1<u>5</u> 3. 11.<u>1</u>8 5. 65.<u>5</u>6 7. 50.<u>6</u>3

2. 10.<u>9</u>3 4. 9.<u>9</u>5 6. 19.<u>8</u>1 8. 19.<u>5</u>8

Underline the digit in the hundredths place.

9. 19.6<u>2</u> 11. 6.7<u>8</u> 13. 73.1<u>7</u> 15. 35.1<u>8</u>

10. 25.8<u>4</u> 12. 22.1<u>5</u> 14. 99.9<u>9</u> 16. 18.3<u>3</u>

Write the place value of the 6 in each number.

17. 16.85 ones 20. 18.65 tenths 23. 93.06 hundredths 26. 45.6 tenths

18. 11.63 tenths 21. 68.19 tens 24. 15.64 tenths 27. 63.05 tens

19. 9.56 hundredths 22. 26.51 ones 25. 6.19 ones 28. 46.51 ones

54 Total Problems: Total Correct: Score: © Carson-Dellosa CD-2210

Worksheet 55 — Reading and Writing Decimals

Name _____ Reading and Writing Decimals

Study the example below. Read each problem. Then, write the number in decimal form on the line provided.

Example:
six and five-tenths is written **6.5**

1. two-tenths .2
2. five-tenths .5
3. nine-hundredths .09
4. six-hundredths .06
5. three and one-tenth 3.1
6. seven-tenths .7

7. one and nine-hundredths 1.09
8. four and six-tenths 4.6
9. fifteen and eight-hundredths 15.08
10. ninety-three-hundredths .93
11. seventeen-hundredths .17
12. three and eleven-hundredths 3.11

Study the examples below. Read each problem. Then, write the decimal in word form on the line provided.

Examples:	
1.8 = **one and eight-tenths**	0.56 = **fifty-six-hundredths**

13. 0.6 six-tenths
14. 0.06 six-hundredths
15. 2.8 two and eight-tenths
16. 0.13 thirteen-hundredths
17. 0.35 thirty-five-hundredths
18. 4.04 four and four-hundredths
19. 0.9 nine-tenths

20. 0.02 two-hundredths
21. 4.17 four and seventeen-hundredths
22. 0.57 fifty-seven-hundredths
23. 5.57 five and fifty-seven-hundredths
24. 0.5 five-tenths
25. 0.1 one-tenth
26. 2.12 two and twelve-hundredths

© Carson-Dellosa CD-2210   Total Problems: Total Correct: Score: **55**

Worksheet 56 — Comparing and Ordering Decimals

Name _____ Comparing and Ordering Decimals

Study the box below. Compare the decimals using < , > , or =. Place the correct symbol in each square.

Rule:	Example:	1.3	☐	1.4
To compare two or more decimals:				
Line up the decimal points.	$\left.\begin{array}{l}1.3\\1.4\end{array}\right\}$ 3 is less than 4, so			
Compare digits from left to right in their corresponding place value positions.	1.3 $<$ 1.4			

1. 0.6 $<$ 0.7
2. 2.3 $=$ 2.3
3. 0.72 $>$ 0.67
4. 4.3 $<$ 4.5

5. 0.6 $=$ 0.60
6. 0.45 $>$ 0.39
7. 0.52 $>$ 0.25
8. 7.6 $=$ 7.60

Order the decimals from least to greatest.

9. 0.5 0.4 0.2
   0.2 0.4 0.5

10. 3.7 3.5 3.8
    3.5 3.7 3.8

11. 30.7 28.4 29.1
    28.4 29.1 30.7

12. 0.62 0.63 0.4
    0.4 0.62 0.63

13. 0.86 0.6 1.3
    0.6 0.86 1.3

14. 9.9 9 9.99
    9 9.9 9.99

56 Total Problems: Total Correct: Score: © Carson-Dellosa CD-2210

Name _____ Adding and Subtracting Decimals

Study the box below. Then, solve the problems and write the answers in the space provided.

Rule:	Example:
1. Line up the decimal points.	3.76 + 1.59 =
2. Start from the far right.	3.76 3.76 3.76
3. Regroup as needed.	+ 1.59 + 1.59 + 1.59
4. Bring the decimal point down to the answer.	5 35 5.35

1. 6.5
 + 7.3
 13.8

2. 2.7
 + 4.1
 6.8

3. 6.5
 − 1.2
 5.3

4. 3.8
 − 2.7
 1.1

5. 0.2
 + 0.5
 0.7

6. 5.9
 − 2.5
 3.4

7. 12.5
 + 9.4
 21.9

8. 0.42
 + 0.36
 0.78

9. 9.8
 − 7.3
 2.5

10. 6.7
 − 4.7
 2.0

11. 2.41
 + 7.49
 9.90

12. 5.7
 + 8.5
 14.2

13. 3.8
 + 4.9
 8.7

14. 0.59
 − 0.18
 0.41

15. 3.86
 + 1.39
 5.25

16. 10.5
 − 7.7
 2.8

17. 4.13
 − 2.95
 1.18

18. 0.28
 + .87
 1.15

19. 4.79
 + 5.75
 10.54

20. 1.2
 − 0.5
 0.7

© Carson-Dellosa CD-2210

| Total Problems: | Total Correct: | Score: | **57** |

Name _____ Problem Solving with Decimals

Solve the word problems. Show your work and write the answers in the space provided.

1. Camilla was taking a math test. Her teacher asked her to write the decimal two and three tenths. She wrote **2.03**. Did she write the decimal correctly? If not, correct it.

 No: 2.3

2. Write thirteen and sixty-three-hundredths. Circle the digit in the tenths place.

 13.(6)3

3. Complete the next 3 decimals in each sequence.

 A. .15, .25, .35, .45, **.55**, **.65**, **.75**

 B. 3.8, 3.7, 3.6, 3.5, **3.4**, **3.3**, **3.2**

4. Place the following numbers in order from least to greatest.

 2.5, 5.2, 4.2, 4.12, 5.25

 2.5; 4.12; 4.2; 5.2; 5.25

5. Mrs. Watson bought each of her two children a bag of popcorn at the movies for $0.79 per bag. How much money did she spend in all for the popcorn?

 .79
 + .79
 $1.58

6. Write twenty and seventy hundredths. Circle the digit in the tenths place.

 20.(7)0

7. Using the greater than (>) and less than (<) symbols, write two number sentences with the following numbers.

 3.4, 3.5

 3.4 < 3.5

 3.5 > 3.4

8. Chuck's weekly allowance is $5.00. After buying a package of beef jerky for $1.67, how much money does he have left?

 $5.00
 − 1.67
 $3.33

| **58** | Total Problems: | Total Correct: | Score: | © Carson-Dellosa CD-2210 |

Name _____ Time to the Quarter Hour

Read each clock. Using numerals, write the time on the line provided. Remember to correctly label each clock with A.M. or P.M.

1. Wake Up

 7:00 A.M.

2. School Starts
 8:15
 8:15 A.M.

3. Bedtime
 8:45
 8:45 P.M.

4. Lunch
 12:00 P.M.

5. Recess
 10:30 A.M.

6. Baseball Game
 5:15 P.M.

7. Reading Group
 2:15
 2:15 P.M.

8. Swim Lesson
 4:45 P.M.

9. Dinner
 7:00
 7:00 P.M.

© Carson-Dellosa CD-2210

| Total Problems: | Total Correct: | Score: | **59** |

Name _____ Elapsed Time

Find each time. All times are A.M. Write the answer on the line provided.

1. 30 minutes after

 5:30 A.M.

2. 15 minutes after
 11:45 A.M.

3. 15 minutes after
 5:00 A.M.

4. 30 minutes after
 3:15 A.M.

5. 30 minutes before
 8:15 A.M.

6. 1 hour before

 4:00 A.M.

7. 30 minutes after 7:05 P.M. **7:35 P.M.**

8. 20 minutes after 9:10 A.M. **9:30 A.M.**

9. 1 hour and 30 minutes before 3:15 P.M. **1:45 P.M.**

10. 45 minutes after 2:15 P.M. **3:00 P.M.**

11. 1 hour after 1:30 P.M. **2:30 P.M.**

12. 45 minutes before 4:15 P.M. **3:30 P.M.**

13. 1 hour and 15 minutes after 9:10 A.M. **10:25 A.M.**

14. 30 minutes after 3:45 P.M. **4:15 P.M.**

| **60** | Total Problems: | Total Correct: | Score: | © Carson-Dellosa CD-2210 |

© Carson-Dellosa CD-2210

Name _____ Reading a Calendar

Mrs. Simms has 2 children, Jay and Joy. The calendar shows Jay's baseball games and Joy's soccer games in April. Use the calendar to answer the questions.

April

Sunday	Monday	Tuesday	Wednesday	Thursday	Friday	Saturday
		1 Jay's Game	2	3 Joy's Game	4	5 Jay's & Joy's Games
6	7 Jay's Game	8 Joy's Game	9	10 Joy's Game	11	12 Jay's Game
13 Jay's Game	14	15 Jay's Game	16	17 Joy's Game	18	19 Jay's & Joy's Games
20	21	22 Jay's Game	23	24 Joy's Game	25 Joy's Game	26 Jay's Game
27	28	29 Jay's Game	30			

1. Who plays the first game of the month?
   Jay

2. What day of the week is the first game?
   Tuesday

3. Who has more games, Jay or Joy?
   Both have 9.

4. Who has a game on the second Tuesday of the month?
   Joy

5. On April 24, Joy has a game. What day of the week is that?
   Thursday

6. How many games does Joy play on Tuesdays and Saturdays?
   _4_

7. On which dates do both Jay and Joy have games?
   April 5 and 19

8. A week begins on Sunday and ends on Saturday. In which week are the most games played?
   the week of April 13

9. Are there any days of the week in which no games are played?
   yes, Wednesday

© Carson-Dellosa CD-2210 | Total Problems: | Total Correct: | Score: | **61**

Name _____ Problem Solving with Time

Solve the word problems. Show your work and write the answers in the space provided.

1. Maya's class ate lunch at 12:00 P.M. If they had 30 minutes to eat, what time did they finish?
   _12:30 P.M._

2. Is the following statement true or false? If false, rewrite it correctly. When it is 10:30, the hour hand is between the 9 and 10.
   False
   When it is 10:30, the hour hand is between the 10 and 11.

3. Malcolm went to play at a friend's house. He left at 4:00 P.M. and was told to be home in 1½ hours. What time should he arrive home?
   _5:30 P.M._

4. Ayesha's baby brother was born at 12:45 P.M. on 7/11/90. Was he born before or after noon? What month and year was he born?
   after noon
   July, 1990

5. Daria's birthday party lasted 2 hours and 30 minutes. The party ended at 4:00 P.M. What time did it begin?
   _1:30 P.M._

6. David took his dogs on a walk from 5:30 to 6:15. Was that less than 1 hour or more than 1 hour?
   less

62 | Total Problems: | Total Correct: | Score: | © Carson-Dellosa CD-2210

Name _____ Adding and Subtracting Money

Add or subtract each problem. Remember to include a decimal point (.) and a dollar sign ($) or a cent sign (¢) in each answer. Write the answer in the space provided.

1. $4.55
    + 0.12
    $4.67

2. $6.70
    − 0.50
    $6.20

3. 65¢
    + 25¢
    90¢

4. $10.30
    − 10.10
    $0.20

5. $5.05
    + 6.13
    $11.18

6. $8.88
    − 7.77
    $1.11

7. $7.95
    + 5.05
    $13.00

8. 89¢
    − 64¢
    25¢

9. $6.45
    + 3.60
    $10.05

10. $5.10
    − 4.90
    $0.20

11. $63.89
    + 12.55
    $76.44

12. $19.85
    − 10.70
    $9.15

13. $29.99
    + 13.95
    $43.94

14. $57.00
    + 19.75
    $76.75

15. $29.53
    + 18.19
    $47.72

16. $151.09
    − 16.10
    $134.99

17. $905.00
    − 675.60
    $229.40

18. $590.50
    + 195.50
    $786.00

19. $619.00
    + 225.53
    $844.53

20. $475.00
    − 199.99
    $275.01

21. $672.00
    − 480.65
    $191.35

22. $781.50
    − 781.39
    $0.11

23. $499.75
    + 399.75
    $899.50

24. $650.03
    + 185.07
    $835.10

© Carson-Dellosa CD-2210 | Total Problems: | Total Correct: | Score: | **63**

Name _____ Making Change under $1

Using only pennies, nickels, dimes, and quarters, what is the fewest number of coins that will make each amount below? Write the answer on the line provided.

1. $0.30 __2__ coins
2. $0.10 __1__ coins
3. $0.45 __3__ coins
4. $0.70 __4__ coins
5. $0.62 __5__ coins
6. $0.38 __5__ coins
7. $0.85 __4__ coins
8. $0.90 __5__ coins
9. $0.98 __8__ coins

Solve the word problems. Show your work and write the answers in the space provided.

10. Rebekah rented a movie that cost $3.79. She gave the clerk $4.00. What was her change?
    $4.00
    − 3.79
    $0.21

11. Rachel bought a magazine for $1.98. She gave the clerk $2.00. What was her change?
    $2.00
    − 1.98
    $0.02

12. Rob bought an action figure for his collection. He gave the clerk a $20 bill for the $19.75 figure. What was his change?
    $20.00
    − 19.75
    $0.25

13. Mark bought a pack of gum for $0.35 and a candy bar for $0.45. He gave the clerk $1.00. What was his change?
    $0.35 $1.00
    + 0.45   − 0.80
    $0.80   **$0.20**

14. Leigh purchased a doll for $19.59. She gave the clerk $20.00. What was her change?
    $20.00
    − 19.59
    $0.41

15. Seth bought a soda from the vending machine. It was $0.55. He put in 3 quarters. What was his change?
    $0.75
    − 0.55
    $0.20

64 | Total Problems: | Total Correct: | Score: | © Carson-Dellosa CD-2210

© Carson-Dellosa CD-2210

Name _____ Making Change over $1

Read the problems below. Then, circle the letter beside the correct amount of change.

1. Erin gave the clerk $10.00 for a hair clip that cost $7.95.

   A. $1.05   B. $2.05   C. $3.05   *(B circled)*

2. Lance gave the clerk $5.00 for an item that cost $3.50.

   A. $1.50   B. $2.50   C. $3.50   *(A circled)*

3. Lamont gave the clerk $5.00 for groceries that cost $3.99.

   A. $0.01   B. $1.01   C. $2.01   *(B circled)*

4. Carrie gave the clerk $20.00 for a shirt that cost $16.78.

   A. $3.12   B. $3.22   C. $4.22   *(B circled)*

5. Tameka gave the clerk $25.00 for a jumper that cost $22.59.

   A. $2.41   B. $2.51   C. $2.61   *(A circled)*

6. Ada gave the cashier $30.00 for a board game that cost $22.71.

   A. $6.29   B. $7.19   C. $7.29   *(C circled)*

7. Lily gave the cashier $50.00 for a phone that cost $29.50.

   A. $11.50   B. $20.50   C. $21.50   *(B circled)*

8. George gave the cashier $100.00 for a painting that cost $71.85.

   A. $28.15   B. $28.05   C. $38.15   *(A circled)*

© Carson-Dellosa CD-2210

| Total Problems: | Total Correct: | Score: |

65

Name _____ Problem Solving with Money

Solve the word problems. Show your work and write the answers in the space provided.

1. Andrew has 3 dimes, 3 nickels, and 7 pennies. Does he have enough money to buy a soda for 50¢?

   30¢ + 15¢ + 7¢ = 52¢
   yes

2. Elli had 3 quarters, 1 dime, 2 nickels, and 6 pennies. Did she have more or less than 1 dollar?

   75¢ + 10¢ + 10¢ + 6¢ = $1.01
   more

3. Liz bought popcorn for $1.89, candy for $1.79, and a soda for 99¢. How much money did she spend?

   $1.89 + $1.79 + $.99 = $4.67

4. Karlton has admired a 10-speed bicycle for a few months. So far he has saved $45.75. The bike costs $79. How much more money does he need to purchase the bike?

   $79.00
   − 45.75
   $ 33.25

5. Sarah paid $29.95 for a video game. Her friend Melissa bought the same game for $27.99. How much more did Sarah pay for the game?

   $29.95
   − 27.99
   $ 1.96

6. Tony gave the clerk $1.00 for a cookie that cost 89¢. How much change did Tony receive?

   $1.00
   − 0.89
   $ 0.11

7. Shayla purchased a video game for $33.54. She gave the clerk $35.04. How much change did she receive?

   $35.04
   − 33.54
   $ 1.50

8. Lucia had 3 dollars, 3 quarters, 8 dimes, 5 nickels, and 6 pennies. Did she have more or less than 5 dollars?

   $3.00 + 75¢ + 80¢ + 25¢ + 6¢ =
   $4.86
   less

66 | Total Problems: | Total Correct: | Score: | © Carson-Dellosa CD-2210

Name _____ Metric Length

Using a centimeter ruler, measure each line segment to the nearest centimeter. Write the answer in the space to the right of the segment.

1. _____ 3 cm   4. _____ 5 cm
2. _____ 5 cm   5. __ 1 cm
3. _____ 7 cm   6. _____ 4 cm

Study the box below. Then, answer "yes" or "no" to each question, on the line provided.

Rules:	Example:
1 centimeter (cm) = 10 millimeters (mm)	Is 1 m longer than 120 cm?
1 decimeter (dm) = 10 centimeters	1 m = 100 cm, so 1 meter is not longer than 120 cm.
1 meter (m) = 100 centimeters	Answer: **No**
1 km (km) = 1,000 meters	

7. Is 15 cm longer than 1 dm? yes
8. Is 900 m longer than 1 km? no
9. Is 1 m longer than 1 dm? yes
10. Is 5 mm longer than 1 cm? no
11. Is 2 cm longer than 10 mm? yes
12. Is 5 dm longer than 1 m? no
13. Is 1 m longer than 90 cm? yes
14. Is 20 cm longer than 1 m? no
15. Is 2 km longer than 1,500 m? yes
16. Is 15 dm longer than 1 m? yes

© Carson-Dellosa CD-2210

| Total Problems: | Total Correct: | Score: |

67

Name _____ Customary Length

Using an inch ruler, measure each segment to the nearest inch. Write the answer in the space to the right of the segment.

1. _____ 1 in
2. _____ 2 in
3. _____ 3 in
4. _____ 4 in
5. _____ 5 in
6. _____ 6 in

Study the box below. Then, answer "yes" or "no" to each question on the line provided.

Rules:	Example:
12 inches = 1 foot	Are there 24 inches in 2 feet?
3 feet or 36 inches = 1 yard	If there are 12 inches in 1 foot, then there are 24 inches in 2 feet (12 x 2).
5,280 feet = 1 mile	Answer: **Yes**

7. Are there 3 yards in 1 foot? no
8. Are there 3 feet in 1 yard? yes
9. Are there 38 inches in 1 yard? no
10. Is 1 mile longer than 4,900 feet? yes
11. Is 36 inches equal to 3 feet? yes
12. Is 3 yards longer than 9 feet? no
13. Are there 6 feet in 2 yards? yes
14. Are there 2 miles in 1000 feet? no
15. Are there 12 inches in 1 foot? yes
16. Is 2 feet longer than 1 yard? no

68 | Total Problems: | Total Correct: | Score: | © Carson-Dellosa CD-2210

Metric Capacity and Mass

Name _____

Study the rules below. Then, determine which measurement seems reasonable and circle the answer.

Rules:	
Milliliter (ml) Used to measure very small amounts of liquid	**Liter (l)** 1 liter = 1,000 milliliters Used to measure average amounts of liquid

1. eyedropper
(2 ml)   2 l

2. bucket
10 ml   (10 l)

3. coffee cup
(40 ml)   4 l

4. bathtub
80 ml   (80 l)

5. teaspoon
(3 ml)   3 l

6. teakettle
2 ml   (2 l)

Study the rules below. Then, determine whether each object should be measured in grams or kilograms. Write the answer on the line provided.

Rules:	
Gram (g) Used to measure smaller objects	**Kilogram (kg)** 1kg = 1,000 g Used to measure larger objects

7. paper clip ___grams___

8. dog ___kilograms___

9. chair ___kilograms___

10. empty bucket ___grams___

11. bucket of water ___kilograms___

12. pencil ___grams___

13. watermelon ___kilograms___

14. letter ___grams___

© Carson-Dellosa CD-2210

| Total Problems: | Total Correct: | Score: | **69** |

Customary Capacity and Mass

Name _____

Study the box below. Then, complete each sentence using "more than," "less than," or "equal to." Write the answer on the line provided.

Rules:	Example:
2 cups = 1 pint 2 pints = 1 quart 4 quarts = 1 gallon	If 2 cups = 1 pint, then, 1 cup is __*less than*__ 1 pint.

1. 2 pints are ___equal to___ 1 quart.

2. 3 quarts are ___less than___ 1 gallon.

3. 1 gallon is ___more than___ 1 pint.

4. 2 pints are ___equal to___ 4 cups.

5. 1 pint is ___less than___ 1 quart.

6. 3 cups are ___less than___ 1 quart.

7. 6 pints are ___equal to___ 3 quarts.

8. 8 quarts are ___equal to___ 2 gallons.

Study the rules below. Then, determine whether each object should be measured in pounds or ounces. Write the answer on the line provided.

Rules:	
Ounce (oz) Used to measure smaller objects	**Pound (lb)** Used to measure larger objects

9. piece of cheese ___ounces___

10. set of encyclopedias ___pounds___

11. bookcase ___pounds___

12. pencil ___ounces___

13. plate ___ounces___

14. refrigerator ___pounds___

70 | Total Problems: | Total Correct: | Score: |

© Carson-Dellosa CD-2210

Problem Solving with Measurement

Name _____

Solve the word problems. Show your work and write the answers in the space provided.

1. Miranda's teddy bear has a width of 10 inches and a length of 20 inches. Which measurement is longer than 1 foot?

length or 20 inches

2. Would you use inches, feet, or miles to measure the length of a school bus?

feet

3. If there are 1,000 meters in 1 kilometer, how many meters are in 2 kilometers? Explain how you reached your answer.

2,000 m

1,000 m
x   2
2,000 m

4. Isabella needs 3 gallons of water to make lemonade. If all she has is a 1-quart container to measure the water, how many times will she have to fill the container to get 3 gallons of water? (Hint: 1 gal = 4 qt)

4 x 3 = 12

5. You have two buckets. One bucket holds 6 liters of water, and the other holds 4 liters. How can you use these buckets to measure 2 liters of water?

Fill up the 6-liter bucket; pour water into the 4-liter bucket until it is full. What's left in the 6-liter bucket is 2 liters of water.

6. Lawrence wants 2 lbs of roast beef. The scale reads 14 oz. Does he have enough? If not, how much more does he need? (Hint: 1 lb = 16 oz)

no
18 oz or 1 lb 2 oz

7. A can of soda has 385 ml of liquid. How many cans would you need to have 1 liter of soda? (Hint: 1,000 ml = 1 l)

3 cans

8. The mass of a dollar bill is about 1 g. Would 2,000 dollar bills weigh more or less than 1 kilogram? (Hint: 1 kg = 1,000 g)

more

© Carson-Dellosa CD-2210

| Total Problems: | Total Correct: | Score: | **71** |

Symmetry

Name _____

Study the box below. Then, determine whether each figure has a line of symmetry. If it does, draw it. If it doesn't, write "none" on the line below it.

Rule:	Example:
A line of symmetry cuts a figure in half so that you see exactly the same image on each side of the line.	

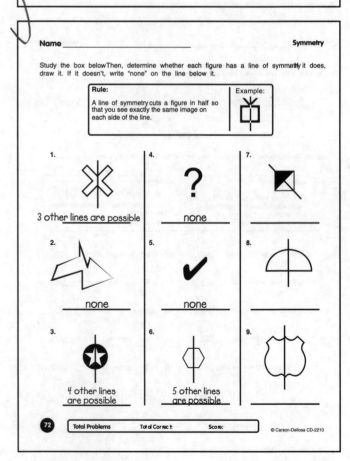

1.
3 other lines are possible

2.
none

3.
4 other lines are possible

4.
none

5.
none

6.
5 other lines are possible

7.

8.

9.

72 | Total Problems | Total Correct: | Score: |

© Carson-Dellosa CD-2210

Page 73

Name _____   **Congruent Figures**

Study the box below. Then, determine whether each pair of figures is congruent. Write "yes" or "no" in the space provided.

Rule:	Examples:
Figures are **congruent** when they have the same size and shape.	congruent not congruent

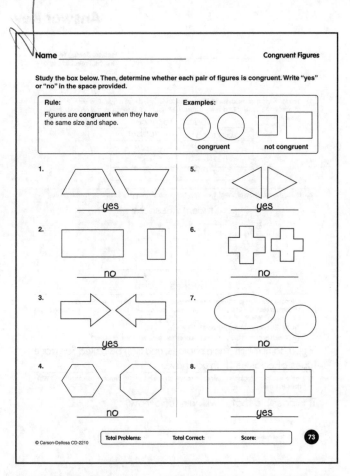

1. yes
2. no
3. yes
4. no
5. yes
6. no
7. no
8. yes

© Carson-Dellosa CD-2210   Total Problems: Total Correct: Score: **73**

Page 74

Name _____   **Lines, Segments, and Rays**

Study the box below. Then, label each figure as a line, segment, or ray. Write the answer on the line provided. Remember to include the points in each answer.

Rules:	Examples:
Line – An endless collection of points along a straight path, named by any two of its points.	E F — Line EF or FE
Segment – A part of a line, named by its two endpoints.	C D — Segment CD or DC
Ray – A part of a line having one endpoint and extending endlessly in one direction, named by the endpoint and one other point.	G H — Ray GH

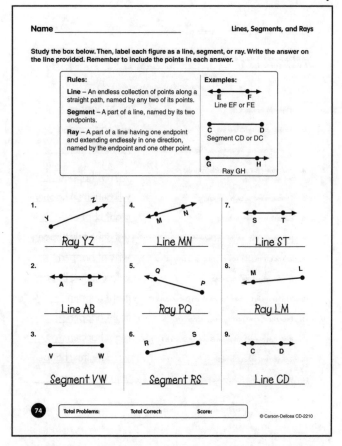

1. Ray YZ
2. Line AB
3. Segment VW
4. Line MN
5. Ray PQ
6. Segment RS
7. Line ST
8. Ray LM
9. Line CD

74   Total Problems: Total Correct: Score: © Carson-Dellosa CD-2210

Page 75

Name _____   **Area and Perimeter**

Study the box below. Then, find the area and perimeter of each figure. Write the answer on the line provided.

Rules:	Examples:
Area (A) is the number of square units inside a figure. To find the area of rectangles and squares, multiply the length times the width.	3
Perimeter (P) is the number of units around a figure. To find the perimeter of rectangles and squares, add the number of squares on each side.	4 — A = 4 x 3 = **12 square units** P = 4 + 3 + 4 + 3 = **14 units**

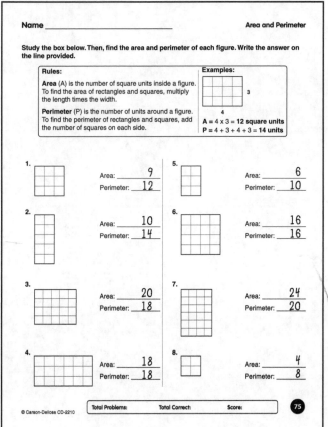

1. Area: 9   Perimeter: 12
2. Area: 10   Perimeter: 14
3. Area: 20   Perimeter: 18
4. Area: 18   Perimeter: 18
5. Area: 6   Perimeter: 10
6. Area: 16   Perimeter: 16
7. Area: 24   Perimeter: 20
8. Area: 4   Perimeter: 8

© Carson-Dellosa CD-2210   Total Problems: Total Correct: Score: **75**

Page 76

Name _____   **Making Tables and Graphs**

Using the data in the box below, make a table in the space provided.

Tips:	Data:
You should have two columns: *Type of Pet* and *Number Owned*. Give the table a title that clearly describes the information shown in the table.	This is a list of pets owned by the students in Rachel's class: dog, dog, dog, cat, bird, cat, cat, bird, fish, bird, guinea pig, dog, dog, dog, cat, bird.

Pets Owned by Students in Rachel's Class

Type of Pet	Number
dog	6
cat	4
bird	4
guinea pig	1
fish	1

Using the table you've made above, make a bar graph in the space provided to display the information.

Tips:	
1. Label the left side (y-axis) and bottom (x-axis).	3. Draw the bars.
2. Choose numbers so that all the data will fit.	4. Give the graph a title which describes the information shown.

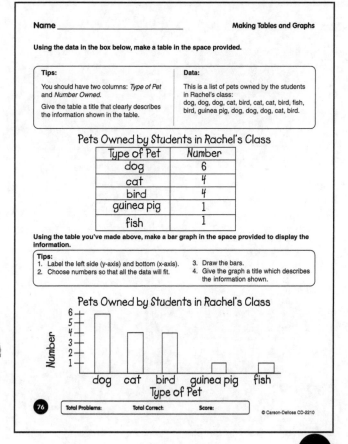

Pets Owned by Students in Rachel's Class

76   Total Problems: Total Correct: Score: © Carson-Dellosa CD-2210

Name _____   Outcomes

Study the rule below. Decide whether the following outcomes are certain (will definitely happen), possible (might happen), or impossible (will not happen). Then, write the answer on the line provided.

> **Rule:**
> An outcome is the result of an event.

1. It will rain tomorrow.   might happen

2. You will grow to 50 feet tall.   will not happen

3. The Falcons will win the Super Bowl next season.   might happen

4. In a drawer full of black socks, you will pick out a white pair.   will not happen

5. Tomorrow will be 24 hours long.   will definitely happen

6. Humans will travel to Mars.   might happen

7. New Year's Eve will fall on December 31ˢᵗ.   will definitely happen

8. In a box of raisins, you will pick out a peanut.   will not happen

9. Ice will make your drink cold.   will definitely happen

10. It will snow in Denver, Colorado, on December 21ˢᵗ.   might happen

11. Every kernel will pop in a bag of popcorn.   might happen

12. It will rain every Monday in Provo, Utah, for a full year.   might happen

13. The sun will set in the west.   will definitely happen

14. Water will boil at 50 degrees Fahrenheit.   will not happen

© Carson-Dellosa CD-2210 | Total Problems: | Total Correct: | Score: | **77**

Name _____   Problem Solving with Data, Graphs, Probability, and Statistics

Solve the word problems in the space provided.

1. The following data indicates student absences for one day at a typical school: 6ᵗʰ grade – 13 absent; 7ᵗʰ grade – 9 absent; 8ᵗʰ grade – 9 absent. Use this information to make a table.

Student Absences

Grades	Number
6	13
7	9
8	9

2. Using the data from problem 1, make a bar graph showing the absences in each grade.

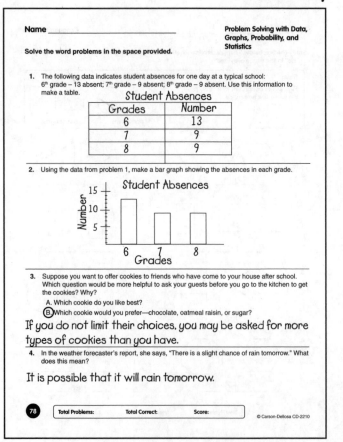

3. Suppose you want to offer cookies to friends who have come to your house after school. Which question would be more helpful to ask your guests before you go to the kitchen to get the cookies? Why?
   A. Which cookie do you like best?
   B. Which cookie would you prefer—chocolate, oatmeal raisin, or sugar?

   If you do not limit their choices, you may be asked for more types of cookies than you have.

4. In the weather forecaster's report, she says, "There is a slight chance of rain tomorrow." What does this mean?

   It is possible that it will rain tomorrow.

78 | Total Problems: | Total Correct: | Score: | © Carson-Dellosa CD-2210